FROM
CHAOS
to
CONFIDENCE

Survival Strategies for the New Workplace

Susan M. Campbell, Ph.D.

A FIRESIDE BOOK
Published by Simon & Schuster

FIRESIDE
Rockefeller Center
1230 Avenue of the Americas
New York, NY 10020

First Fireside Edition 1996

FIRESIDE and colophon are registered trademarks
of Simon & Schuster Inc.

Designed by Bonni Leon

Manufactured in the United States of America

10   9   8   7   6   5   4   3   2

Library of Congress Cataloging-in-Publication Data
Campbell, Susan M.
   From chaos to confidence : survival strategies for the
new workplace / Susan Campbell.
      p.   cm.
   Includes bibliographical references.
   1. Career development.   2. Organizational change.
3. Job satisfaction.   I. Title.
HF5549.5.C35C34   1995
650.1—dc20   95-13727
                                                   CIP

ISBN: 0-684-80253-8
ISBN: 0-684-80252-X (pbk)

To my parents,
who taught me to trust
the movement
from chaos to confidence
and back again to chaos.

ACKNOWLEDGMENTS

Many people have been involved in the insemination, incubation, and midwifery of this book. I feel deeply grateful to so many friends, colleagues, clients, mentors, and other authors, who generously shared with me their stories and experiences. I want to especially thank Jordan Paul for his help in thinking through and preparing the material on building trust and respect in Chapter Seven. Thanks also to: Peller Marion, Ron Tilden, Kenn Burrows, Arlene Scott, Pat Neuman, John O'Neil, John Adams, Peter Russell, Jim Simonds, Stanley Russell, Milton Friedman, Dale Ironson, Doug Ross, Lee Shapiro, Brent Whipple, Sara Byrnes, and John Enright.

The team responsible for the book's production and publication deserve special recognition. They include my editor at Simon and Schuster, Becky Cabaza, and my agent, Ray Bard.

And, finally, I want to acknowledge the very special role played by my dad, Harry Campbell. For the entire two years the book was being written, he kept me abreast of the latest books and journal articles related to my subject, sending me Xeroxed articles and handwritten book reviews almost monthly. I am blessed to have a father who cares deeply about making this world a better place for all.

CONTENTS

FROM
CHAOS
to
CONFIDENCE

Our Collective Crisis

American organizations cannot evolve any farther than the individuals who work in these organizations. If we want our institutions to be more change-worthy, individual workers will need to undertake the personal learning necessary to perceive change as it is happening.

"*I never thought it would happen to me. I've been downsized. My project was one of the hottest in the company. I thought I had the support of top management. But a month ago last Friday, they told me it was my last day. What I remember most about that day is that no one came over to me to say goodbye. It was like I was all of a sudden an untouchable—like if they got near me they might be next. Or maybe they just didn't know what to say.*"

"*I'm CEO around here, so people think I have a lot of power. Well, it doesn't feel like it. I have to keep everyone else happy. I have made so many commitments to people that I'm afraid I can't fulfill—employment contracts, benefits packages. If I renege on my word, I lose my credibility. But if I don't do something to cut costs, we'll fold.*"

"*They told me I have to lay off forty people during the next year. I don't know if I can do it. Some of these folks have been my friends for fifteen years. And the irony of it is, it's possible that the day after I send the last person on his way, I could be gone just like them.*"

"I'm afraid to tell my manager that our team is having problems working together. There's this one guy that nobody can get along with. I doubt if my manager would be much help anyway. He's not much of a communicator. He doesn't realize what it takes to build relationships you can really depend on."

"We use a lot of temps now. They come in for a few months, and then they're gone. I got real close to one woman. We had a lot in common and liked each other a lot. We took walks together during our lunch break. Then one day she wasn't there, and I found out her contract was up. I had no warning or preparation. She was just gone. We never talked about that."

"This job is killing me. There's just too much to do. I can never get caught up. I always feel someone breathing down my neck. I'm afraid to ask for help because my manager is so unsympathetic. She expects everyone to overwork themselves the way she does. What are we doing to ourselves?"

Everywhere we look, we see evidence that the American workplace is in crisis. Most of us are working harder now to maintain the same standard of living that we had ten years ago. Every day we hear of another company laying off part of its workforce. Stress disability claims are at an all-time high. We are living in exceedingly uncertain times—where promises are made and then broken, and anything you have today may be gone tomorrow.

This is our collective crisis. No one is immune from its effects. Even if you feel economically secure, even if your job is not endangered, you are still affected by the collective premonition that things cannot and will not go on as they always have. We have entered a new era. The Age of Uncertainty. The Age of Chaos. The Age of Nonstop, Ever-Accelerating Change.

There has never been a time like this in human civilization. We humans have achieved the technological capacity to both create life and to destroy ourselves. We know more and can do more than any other civilization in recorded history. Yet according to public opinion surveys, we feel out of touch with our bodies, overstressed or frustrated in our work, and isolated from our communities and families.

Clearly, something isn't right with the way things are going. Our accustomed ways of thinking, perceiving, and conducting business do not work for us anymore. But we are reluctant to admit that the old ways are not working. It is only natural to fear that if we do face the need for change, we might feel overwhelmed with anxiety and uncertainty. Or we might lose what we have worked so hard to achieve. Change nearly always involves discomfort and fear. It requires us to let go of what's familiar and step into the unknown. So while our old ways are no longer working, we have not yet discovered a better way.

This book offers a new vision regarding the nature and purpose of human work. It offers guidance in how to use crisis as a catalyst for personal and organizational change. I feel strongly that the collective crisis we now face can truly be a collective opportunity. Managers, leaders, employees, entrepreneurs, and people in transition—we are being called to learn new ways of working, and even to discover new and deeper *reasons* for working. "Making a living" is not really why we work. We work to "make ourselves." I believe that we have an innate desire to complete ourselves as we go through life's journey. We want to know who we are and what our purpose is. We want to offer what we have to others and be acknowledged for what we have given. We want to join with others in communities where people help each other refine our gifts.

In these uncertain and turbulent times, workers need to discover a more abiding sense of the purpose for their work—one that embraces transience. As we attempt to come to terms with the truism that "nothing's for certain, nothing's for sure," we need to find meaning in this dilemma. Without some deeper sense of why we work, we will not survive in the new workplace.

As the world around us becomes more and more complex, we are called on to adapt and learn, not just as individuals but also as communities, teams, or partnerships. Most workers now spend nearly half their time in collaborative relationships in which decisions need to be made jointly. Yet most companies offer no training in how to work as a team. Some people who are quite effective working solo have difficulty working in a group.

Self-managing teams are becoming the basic building blocks of America's larger organizations. Such teams are empowered to solve problems and implement decisions with little or no intervention by management. If a self-managing team is to do its job, team members need to be able to build consensus out of disagreement. Members are expected to set aside personal agendas in favor of the group mission. Yet conflicts must be aired and honored. Teamwork is a constant balancing act between self-interest and group interest. This calls for a very complex set of communication skills.

The Learning Organization

In a workplace where change is the rule rather than the exception, we need new organizational structures and new leadership models as well as new personal attitudes and strategies. The new workplace requires us to go beyond vision and rhetoric to an entirely new experience of what it means to be a worker and what it means to be an organization.

Workers used to earn their sense of value by producing goods and offering services. Now your value in an organization is measured by your ability to respond to change. Today's worker faces the threat of obsolescence every day.

How do we deal realistically with the pressures to constantly develop new skills, to do more with less, to build instant rapport with strangers, and to let go quickly of people and projects to which we have grown attached? There are no easy answers to these questions. We are all exploring this frontier together. A partial answer lies in recreating our major social institutions as learning communities or learning organizations—systems where people are constantly upgrading their resources and updating one other about their current reality.

Since January 1993, every issue of the *Harvard Business Review* has contained at least one article referring to the concept of "the learning organization." Management gurus like Tom Peters and Peter Senge are urging managers to create teams and organizations that can learn and even create knowledge together. Former Citicorp chairman Walter Wriston, in his recent book, *The Twilight of Sovereignty,* reminds us that a company's competitive advantage now lies in its ability to attract and develop its workers' "intellectual capital." While some people may be put off by some of the jargon surrounding these ideas, learning is not simply the latest business buzzword. Re-creating our organizations as learning communities is a lasting and viable solution to the problem of nonstop change. If organizations are to keep from becoming obsolete, they will need employees for whom learning is a way of life, even a passion, not just something we do at training seminars.

If you work in a large organization, or if you read any of the popular business magazines, you have undoubtedly run into terms like *continuous improvement, team learning, organizational learning,* and *knowledge workers.* As these terms imply, today's company is becoming as much a school as a place where things are produced. And today's worker is as much a learner as a producer. In a learning organization, making yourself is as important as making a living. Making yourself is a lifelong process of conscious self-discovery and creation. You use everything that happens in your work and in the rest of your life to assist you in realizing your full potential. A learning organization is made up of learning organisms— people committed to making themselves while making a living. The organizational forms are already emerging that support the idea of making ourselves.

Learning is and always has been the essential activity of every truly successful person and group. It is the key to survival in the new workplace. Workers who thrive will be those who commit themselves to lifelong learning. Managers whose careers self-renew rather than self-destruct will be those who understand how people learn and who become consummate learners themselves. To be continually *making yourself* means that you are continually open to learning from whatever life offers you.

Organizational change is unpredictable. Trying to foresee what is ahead and plan for it doesn't work anymore. We must create entirely new organizational processes, processes that put all aspects of the organization, including its environment, in immediate interactive communication with one another. This means you will be communicating daily with people from a variety of fields, including some whose values or work styles will feel foreign or threatening. You will also learn from and with these people.

Learning will form the foundation of the new organization. Learning expands our capabilities. It always involves a relationship between the known and the unknown, the familiar and the strange, the self and the other. It requires tolerating the discomfort caused by discrepancies between what you believe and what someone else believes or between what you know and what you need to know. In learning we are changed through our relationship with the other. Through interacting with others, we develop a more adequate, more complex response to the situation. This often involves looking beneath the facts as presented for the beliefs or assumptions underlying the facts, and updating those assumptions based on current reality. Learning brings about a shift in paradigms.

We might think of ourselves as surfers riding the waves of change. The successful surfer is one who stays just ahead of the wave that could wipe him out at any moment. He uses the power of this very same wave, participating with it, not fighting it or trying to control it—interacting with its every nuance in the most intimate manner. In order to ride that ever-changing wave, he must also be in good communication with his own body and feelings. His senses and his emotions must give him accurate, undistorted information. Both his internal communications and his communications with his environment are functioning at a high level of clarity. He is a finely tuned instrument for learning from experience.

This is what we all need to become in order to survive and thrive in the new workplace—finely tuned change and learning instruments. We must learn to relate to our environment instead of trying to control it. When we learn to base our decisions on the principle of *relationship* instead of *control,* we pay attention to the moment-to-moment communications between all relevant parties.

New organizational forms are emerging that put each person in a feedback loop where her ideas, thoughts and feelings can be more quickly and readily heard, learned from, and updated. This means changing the unwritten rules in our organizations and changing how workers perceive themselves. It could mean, for example, inviting people from various levels in the organization to sit down together in a meeting that used to be attended only by officers. It will undoubtedly mean that leaders need to get comfortable sharing decision-making with people who have no special rank or position. It will mean sharing information with colleagues working on similar problems instead of keeping important discoveries to yourself to protect your turf. It will also mean focusing more energy on trying new things and less on trying to look good in the boss's eyes. It will probably mean adopting a more pragmatic, less personal, attitude toward failures and mistakes—an attitude that encourages us to admit our errors as quickly as possible so that we can perceive other options. It clearly means changing our personal mind-sets about how we work and why we work. If the capacity for learning is the new competitive resource, a commitment to making yourself while you're making a living is the means to continued survival.

Being open to continually making and remaking yourself requires a level of self-trust and trust in life that most people cannot even imagine. The six meta-skills described in Part Two give us a foundation for developing such trust.

How to Best Use This Book

This book is a self-study course designed to help you stretch your comfort zone and build new capacities. These new capacities will help you become aware of how open you are to novelty and change, how you resist change, and how you can grow beyond these resistances at your own pace.

At various points in the text, you will find self-help activities, called "Meta-Skill Builders." Many of these require written responses, so you will need to have paper and pen nearby as you read.

At the ends of Chapters Four through Nine, the main ideas of the chapters are summarized under the headings "How This Meta-Skill Can Help You Become Indispensible to Your Organization and Customers" and "How This Meta-Skill Can Help You Prevent or Respond to Crisis." The former of the two is designed to help you to be more effective where you currently are in the workplace. The latter section presupposes that in the coming years, there may be a major, potentially traumatic, shift in the way business is conducted, not only in our own country but throughout the world. Many futurists are predicting cataclysmic changes in the present economic system. If such major shifts occur, those who survive will be those of us who have the ability to creatively adapt to change, to let go of what is no longer useful, to build strong alliances with others, and to create order out of complexity. When you master these meta-skills, you increase your chances of surviving whatever evolutionary upheavals the future may have in store.

Throughout the book are stories from the lives of people who have struggled to find a balance between control and openness to learning. As you read these stories, compare your story to theirs, looking both for parallels and differences.

See if you can bring your whole self into the reading process—your feelings as well as your thoughts, your confusion as well as your certainty, your challenging questions as well as your points of agreement with the ideas presented. This way, reading can be an active self-discovery process.

from
SECURITY/
CONTROL
to
LEARNING/
DISCOVERY

CHAPTER ONE

To Control or to Learn?
That Is the Question!

Life is a continual process of growth and change. It is possible to prepare ourselves to be constantly surprised by life, so that we can deal with things as they come up instead of waiting to be knocked down by a crisis. We can learn to perceive the subtler, early-warning signs of impending crisis if we can let go of the idea that we live in an orderly and predictable universe. There is a way to maintain an overall sense of balance without resorting to outdated notions of order and stability.

Much of what I know about coping with crisis, change, and conflict I learned from my blue-water cruising experiences. Sailing the world's oceans for several years of my adult life has given me a deep appreciation for the importance of paying careful attention to what is going on around me—and adapting my actions to fit what is actually going on. Perhaps this sounds simple and obvious. I wish it were as easy as it is obvious.

Let me illustrate with an incident from my most recent sailing expedition.

It was a calm and balmy day as our small craft scudded along effortlessly on our voyage from Mexico to French Polynesia. Then the wind died down to almost nothing as it often does in that part of the ocean known as the doldrums. In an effort to keep up our speed, we decided to put up the spinnaker. It was going to be my job to handle the winch on the yacht's central mast, letting the sheets out gradually while the captain used the spinnaker pole to position the sail. With both hands on the spinnaker sheet, I was about to tie it off when all of a sudden the wind picked up. I wasn't prepared for that unexpected blast of wind, and before I knew what was happening, the sheet was off the winch and in my hands alone. The only thing keeping that enormous sail from dropping into the ocean was my two bare hands.

There was the force of the wind pulling the sail in one direction, away from the boat, and then there was me pulling in the other direction. It was my job to keep that sail in the air.

At that point I had a decision to make: should I let go and surrender to the fact that the wind was clearly the more powerful force in the situation, or should I fight to hold on to the sheet? I could not admit that I hadn't given the task my full attention. So I held on —as best I could.

As I was being pulled up the mast, my palms and legs burning from the ropes, I thought, No, this can't be happening!

I was dangling fifteen feet up off the deck before I admitted, "It's happening, and I'd better let go before I get killed." So I fell to the deck, finally willing to admit my error and deal with it.

What a lesson!

What was it that I learned from that attempt to defy the wind?

It's a lesson I've learned many times over and one I'll probably confront again. When life's unwanted surprises catch me unprepared, I can either resist what's happening and conduct business as usual, or I can surrender to things as they are and deal realistically with my predicament.

It is not always easy to find the wisdom to know the difference. In my case, I couldn't let go of that sail because I couldn't surrender to the fact that I'd made a mistake.

This book has grown out of my own search to discover how to open up to the lessons that life is offering me. Most of what I have learned has come to me from my own mistakes. In addition to holding on too long to that spinnaker sheet, I have committed assorted other errors—and learned many lessons—in my roles as wife, stepparent, college professor, small business owner, organizational consultant, psychotherapist, stock market trader, real estate developer, counseling center director, and CEO for a research think tank.

I have also been privileged to learn from others in high places who have allowed me to witness their misadventures. Much of my work involves consulting with executives and business owners—people who are accustomed to being in charge and in control. These are men and women of considerable achievement and personal power. Traditionally, this work has focused on how to ensure their continued success in a rapidly changing marketplace. But recently, my conversations with these executives have become more about managing their anxieties regarding the future and less about planning and forecasting. "We have so little to go on, so little certainty about where the world will be even six months from now. How can we plan anything?" remarked one CEO from a *Fortune* 500 company. "The truth is that planning, in the usual sense of that term, has become a meaningless activity."

This executive went on to report that his own level of stress had just about brought him to the breaking point more than once over the past year. He was finding that he could no longer honor many of the agreements he had made with people inside and outside the company because his industry was changing so fast. Laying people off was heartbreaking. Being forced to stall on payments to some suppliers did not fit his image of integrity. He was used to feeling in control. But he disclosed in a confessional tone, "Now I really don't know what I'm doing most of the time.

"I know my company needs me to articulate a clear and strong vision, but my vision is blurred. I feel as if I'm looking out the window of a fast-moving train at the trees brushing against the side of the car. I long for a view of the villages and hills I know to be out there beyond the trees. But all I can see are those damned trees and bushes. Everything is too close, and it's coming at me so fast. I can't get perspective on the whole thing."

This leader's dilemma is a familiar one: he found himself in unfamiliar territory without a map to guide him, and without enough trust in the unknown to allow him to explore where to go next.

This sort of anxiety is shared by many people no matter what their position in the organization. People don't know anything for sure anymore. I think we have to admit this fact and take a different posture toward *the unknowns* in our life if we are to survive and thrive in the new workplace. We need to learn to admit it when things aren't going as we had planned or predicted. We need to learn to let go of our need to know what is going on and admit that we often do not know. We have to learn to ask for other people's help and input more often and more skillfully. Learning these things will require a period of trial-and-error exploration. As we come to trust the exploration process, we will grow in our ability to trust ourselves. Making ourselves more trustworthy, change-worthy, and learning-worthy—this is the key to our survival.

When an oceangoing vessel is constructed to stay afloat through all kinds of wind and weather, we call it seaworthy. When a person or an organization is so constructed, we call ourselves change-worthy. Like the ocean, life is not something we control. Like the wind, market conditions cannot be predicted and planned for. What we can do is stay open and aware of the feedback we are getting moment to moment. When we become good at doing this, our need to control the uncontrollable lessens, and we grow in our ability to trust, to learn, and to creatively adapt. As a sailor friend of mine used to say, "We can't control the wind, but we can be ever ready to adjust our sails."

Some of us are quite good at accepting things as they are. These people ask: "What does this situation require? Should we increase or decrease our sail area? Should we stay the course or chart a new one?" Others of us find it more difficult to accept and deal with sudden change. We often get caught up in assigning blame or feeling upset. We react: "Why do things have to be this way? How come we're encountering so many storms—this isn't hurricane season!"

In this book, I will contrast two sets of basic assumptions about life. Each set of assumptions leads to a different way of viewing and dealing with life's unwanted surprises. One way of looking at the world says, "The world is basically stable, predictable and in large part controllable. I get my sense of well-being from knowing the rules, from being around others who are similar to me, and from having things turn out more or less as predicted." This worldview I call the Security/Control mind-set.

Such an attitude assumes things will be as they always have been. It is uncomfortable with uncertainty, change, ambiguity, lack of structure, and with people who see things differently. In this mind-set, we are focused on *making a living,* so anything that appears to threaten the status quo will be feared or resisted. Most of us have some attachment to this attitude, even if we are attempting to grow beyond it. Most of our cultural institutions, including marriage, work, parenting, government, and religion, are founded on Security/Control values.

There is another set of assumptions that says, "The world is a complex system of interacting forces, many of which I cannot directly perceive with my five senses. I enjoy experimenting to discover what works and what doesn't. I like the expanded perspective I get from seeing the world through other peoples' eyes. I do not assume that what worked last time will work this time. I get my sense of well-being from staying awake to myself and my surroundings and from the constant learning process that results from paying attention and from moving into unknown territory." I have named this set of attitudes the Learning/Discovery mind-set. In this mind-set, you are focused on *making yourself.*

When you are in the Learning/Discovery mode, you are open to the unexpected. You accept uncertainty, change, ambiguity, diversity, and lack of structure. You appreciate people who are different because of what you can learn from these people. Learning/Discovery gives you a new reason for working. You view your work as a way of developing yourself into a finely tuned instrument for discovering what is really going on and for responding creatively to your environment. Your work is your vehicle for making yourself.

In this attitude, you *relate* to your environment rather than try to *control* it. You are engaged in a continual exchange of feelings and facts, energy and information, with the world around you. This attitude focuses less on what you are losing when something in your life changes, and more on the opportunities for growth created by letting go of the old ways. You probably have at least some ability to operate within the Learning/Discovery framework, perhaps more than you think.

When you approach life from a Security/Control perspective, you often find yourself struggling against forces over which you have little or no influence—the wind, the weather, the clock, the stock market, or other peoples' opinions. When you view change as loss, you automatically resist it more. When you come at things with a Learning/Discovery attitude, you are empowered to deal with them realistically—as I was when I finally got my feet back on the ground after fighting with that spinnaker.

If you are anything like me, you have both of these potentials within you—the tendency to want to control things or get them to come out right, and the wish to learn what this situation has to teach you.

This book is about how to embrace Learning/Discovery as your basic stance in life. From my experiences with people wrestling daily with the forces of change, I have discovered that those who thrive in a constantly changing environment are those who approach problems with more of the Learning/Discovery attitude. This attitude is embodied in the six strategic "meta-skills" described in Part Two of this book.

A meta-skill is more than just the ability to do something. Learning new meta-skills represents the building of new capacities—capacities that allow you to experience life more truly and fully, and to deal with life more serenely and effectively. This is the type of learning that adds to your measure as a human being. Meta-skills are the basic foundational skills of life that enable you to perform other important life activities. They add to your capacity for exchanging feelings and facts, energy and information. Here are those six meta-skills that enable you to live a life of continuous Learning/Discovery:

1. The capacity to feel yourself as a participant in the change process—not as a controller, and not a victim of it (to be explored in Chapter Four)
2. The capacity to let go of how you think things should be so you can see how they really are (Chapter Five)
3. The capacity to express your essential self, your most cherished qualities and gifts, in your work (Chapter Six)
4. The capacity to communicate openly with others, to exchange information and feelings in ways that lead to mutual learning and trust (Chapter Seven)
5. The capacity to *both* stay true to your own viewpoint *and* open to others' views (Chapter Eight)
6. The capacity to learn with others and to feel connected to others in a team effort (Chapter Nine)

These meta-skills are not in-born. They are learned in response to challenges. Each of the six chapters in Part Two describes how to use the crises and conflicts of your life to develop one of these basic abilities, enabling you to live a life of continuous learning, discovery, and self-creation. When you are in the Learning/Discovery mode, you are relaxed, yet attentive and ready for anything. You respond to each new challenge as it appears instead of allowing problems to accumulate and develop into crises.

The Security/Control mind-set does not equip us very well to deal with a world in which change seems out of control. It is too simplistic, unrealistic, and mechanistic. It hangs on too long to our expectations of how things should be, preventing us from seeing how things really are. It does not take into account the fact that everything that happens has more than one cause, that sometimes I can reach a solution without knowing how I got there, and that often when I stop trying so hard to make something happen, that is when it finally happens.

The Learning/Discovery mind-set accepts paradox, uncertainty, complexity, and transience. It offers a new vision about how work gets accomplished and about what people need in order to feel motivated and committed. It is a vision that can help us feel in charge of ourselves even when the things around us are in chaos.

The Control Paradox

We all want a sense of control over our lives, but we are faced with a profound paradox: the more we try to exert control over the events of our lives, the less in control we feel. Security/Control thinking often leaves us feeling frustrated and out of control. The world we live in is not very friendly to the Security/Control-oriented part of our natures. If we are to move gracefully in a world of nonstop change and global interdependence, we must develop an entirely new definition of what it means to be in control.

We must learn to live with the awkwardness of not knowing anything for sure. We must learn to make decisions, not *on the basis of* accurate data, but *in order to obtain* accurate data. We must learn to communicate and negotiate with people whose worldviews seem alien or illogical. We must learn to adapt quickly, while at the same time honoring those who adapt more slowly. We must make *learning* more important than being right, getting the right outcome, or knowing the right thing to do.

I first became conscious of the Learning/Discovery mind-set as an alternative to my usual Security/Control stance in my mid-twenties. I had been a research psychologist in a large organization for about a year—my first "real job"—and it was time for my first official performance appraisal. I had been aware for quite some time that my manager, Bill, and I had very different work styles. He was highly organized and methodical. My style was more free-form and spontaneous. It wasn't always easy for him to perceive the order within my chaos. In spite of our differences, I respected, even idolized, this man. I think I felt inadequate around him, but I did my best to mask these feelings.

On the occasion of this performance appraisal meeting, I was extremely nervous as I anticipated how things might go. Bill looked troubled, almost angry, as he began to speak: "Susan, you have no aptitude for science. Your data-gathering is haphazard and inconsistent. You pay too much attention to your interpretations of the data and not enough attention to the data itself. I'm not sure you belong here." Having grown up in an environment where I received very little criticism or negative feedback, I was devastated by Bill's evaluation. For a long time, maybe two or three minutes, I sat there speechless. My mind was paralyzed. My emotions were numb. Of course, somewhere below my conscious awareness, I was in great pain. But that was something I was not used to feeling —especially in the company of another person. I don't recall what I said after that, but I'm pretty sure it did not reflect my true feelings. I probably tried to get out of there as quickly as possible.

The interesting part of this story is what went on in my mind during the next twenty-four hours. My first thought was, I'll quit my job. I don't want to be where I'm not wanted. Clearly a Security/Control reaction. That would get me back in control quickly and cleanly. When I finally went to bed that night, I didn't sleep much. I recall a few times waking up from a half sleep saying to myself, "This can't be happening. Things like this don't happen to me." Translation: "If I don't know how to handle something, then I'll just pretend it isn't happening."

Finally, at daybreak, a light dawned in my consciousness as well. I saw that this man was telling me something about myself that was true. And here I was about to run the other way—to escape from the pain of seeing myself realistically. It dawned on me right then that I had a choice: to face myself squarely, acknowledge my limitations, and work to grow beyond them; or to continue to put on a happy face, pretending to be who I thought I was supposed to be, and conduct business as usual. I decided to choose the former option, the Learning/Discovery option.

I went to work the next day and asked Bill if he would help me learn to think more like a research scientist. I was full of self-doubts about my ability to live up to this aspiration. Clearly, I would be moving into unknown territory. And if I did not succeed, it would be a public failure as well as a private one. But my commitment to learning was greater than my need to protect myself from failure. I wanted him to help me make myself, not just make a living.

Together we laid out a program of learning goals and strategies. I was to meet with him every week to report on my progress and receive his suggestions and feedback. That next year was pretty humbling for me. I had never been in the posture of *learner* before. Sure, I had been a student for much of my life, but if your education was anything like mine, you know how little of what occurs in school offers a true and deep experience of being personally changed. As a learner, I had to confront the things I didn't know how to do and the ways I didn't know how to be. Then I had to open myself to other ways—ways that did not feel comfortable, ways that brought up self-doubts and fears. In spite of my discomfort, that year was one of the high points of my life. It was the year I began to trust myself. I let go of having to always feel in control, and in the process a new sense of trust was born—trust that I could handle whatever happens to me.

I have since come to realize that trust can only emerge when we let go of control. All true learning involves the awkwardness and discomfort of entering unknown territory. If you're afraid to be uncomfortable, you're not going to learn much.

I have learned to view everything that happens to me, especially the painful or unexpected things, as opportunities to take inventory of myself—to look at what aspects of my life are out of balance or needing attention, and at what outdated or limiting beliefs I am holding that perpetuate this imbalance. Instead of feeling like a bad person when I find something I'm not so good at, I have come to view "inadequacy feelings" as a natural part of being a living, growing human being.

This value on learning and discovery has made it possible for me to face extremely difficult situations in my life without feeling like a victim or a failure. Learning is so much more important than being right or getting things to go your way. When you are committed to learning, you are in touch with life—instead of your fantasies about life.

As I reflect now on why the Learning/Discovery stance is so useful in these times, I think it is because it helps you accept life as it comes, without needing to pretty it up and without wasting energy thinking about what might have been. This makes it possible to see your current situation realistically rather than as you fear it is or wish it were. When you accept things as they are, you feel empowered to do something about them. When you deal in wishes and fears, there's nothing you can do because you are not dealing with current reality.

When I was dangling fifteen feet up off the deck of our yacht, there was nothing I could do to keep that sail from dropping into the ocean. When I surrendered to the situation as it was, I let go of "how things should have been," and was able to do what was necessary to save our spinnaker. The Learning/Discovery posture usually allows for quicker action and decision-making. When you are open to the facts, regardless of whether they fit your wishes and plans, you can get on with what the situation demands.

Learning/Discovery Turns Crisis into Opportunity

Between 1975 and 1989, I made a significant portion of my income from buying, remodeling, and selling single-family homes in California. Then, in early 1990, the market began to change. The state was losing population due to the dismantling of the defense industry. Other major industries were downsizing, leaving people feeling insecure and less willing to take on new home mortgages. I watched the bottom fall out of property values and my carefully nurtured nest egg all but disappear. My plan had been to develop a substantial passive income stream by capitalizing on California's consistently rising real estate prices. By 1990, this plan was obsolete.

As I have stated, there are two ways to react to such a situation: resist it, and try to conduct business as usual, or accept it and learn from it. Like many people when they are caught unprepared, I attempted to conduct business as usual. I stuck to my plan to put one house per year on the market. I stuck to my obsolete projections of what that house would sell for. And I waited for the house to sell, so I could reap some profits and turn them into another project. And I waited. And I waited.

If I had not shifted my stance to one of learning, I might be waiting still. Finally, I could not deny the fact that my old plan was not going to work. The market had changed. The world had changed. I would need to change, too.

From this position of acceptance, I was able to perceive the state's real estate market and demographics more realistically. I realized that my houses might not sell for a very long time, and that I probably would not get my asking price. I was totally unprepared for this situation. I felt helpless and out of control. That was the bad news. The good news was that I was able to accept these feelings. I had no plan. All I had was my ability to stay open and ask questions, without knowing if any answers would come to me.

As I was to learn quite soon, this ability to stay open in the face of bad news is a powerful resource. It was this ability that enabled me to generate new options and get unstuck. It enabled me to see that there were several new developments in the overall California real estate picture that I could use to my advantage, such as lower interest rates and the fact that declining home sales meant a stronger rental market.

So I decided to refinance my properties, lower my monthly payments, and keep the homes for the rental income. This became my new plan, and one that I would pursue until market conditions changed.

Every problem has a solution embedded in it. Every crisis holds within it an opportunity. When I lost faith in this basic life principle and tried to make things come out as planned, I felt like my feet were stuck in concrete. When I accepted my situation and allowed this principle to operate, I could move again.

Once again we see how my attempt to control the uncontrollable led to needless stress and wasted energy. When I opened up to what I could learn from the situation just as it was, I discovered the hidden positive potential in the mishap that had befallen me.

Can you recall the last time you were caught unprepared by one of life's unwanted surprises? Which stance did you take? Did you try to get back in control? Or did you focus on seeing things as they really were? How effective were your efforts? If you had it to do over, would you do things any differently?

Learning/Discovery Sees Change as the Rule, Not the Exception

The Learning/Discovery mind-set helps us take in the constant fluidity of every situation. When we view everything as in the process of changing from something to something else, we adopt a stance of relaxed attention. We gain a more far-reaching view of where we are headed. We stop focusing on every little success or failure and see what is really important in the big picture. We stop trying to control the things that are happening in the marketplace and open up to perceiving the opportunities these events bring.

This represents a profound vision shift—learning to see change, not as some nuisance that happens to you, but as something natural and healthy that you participate in every day of your life.

It can be difficult to update our perceptions about how the world works if everyone around us is still looking through the old lenses. Most of us grew up in a world where change was something that happened occasionally, and then things went back to normal. In those days, we dealt with major disruptions to the status quo once in a blue moon. Life seemed pretty stable and predictable.

We knew what we needed to do to make a profit. Knowing what to do, knowing the answers, knowing the rules has always been very important to American businesses. Our educational system, too, is based on knowing the right answers—not on learning. (Knowing the answers is static. Learning is fluid.) Even our families had as their model "Father Knows Best." Those were the good old days for many of us. The only problem with that worldview was it taught us to be uncomfortable with not knowing. It even taught us to pretend we knew when we did not. It told us that we were inadequate if we felt uncertain or if we did not know the answers. It taught us to fear change.

In the days when really big changes happened more gradually, this belief system didn't hurt us too much. Now, however, the need to be right or know the answer in order to feel okay is dangerous to our survival. It hurts our organizations because we spend entirely too much energy trying to prove ourselves right or appear to know when we do not. This impairs our ability to accurately perceive and deal with the ongoing, ever-changing flow of reality.

For me, the Learning/Discovery attitude has in some ways been an answer to my prayers. It legitimizes the experience of not knowing what to do. It makes it okay, even desirable, to admit to not knowing. It opens my mind to seeing things in new ways, because it supports me in admitting that my habitual ways are no longer adequate. It's not easy to let oneself feel insecure and inept. But at least now, with Learning/Discovery as my model, I can face the unknown with a little more courage.

The Costs of Control, the Benefits of Learning

If we wish to change our lives for the better, we need to let go of what we think we know and allow a fundamental shift to take place in our way of thinking.

In my work, I get to know people deeply. They tell me the secrets that even their loved ones never hear. So I am privileged to see what makes people happy and what makes them hurt. From my observations, there is one personality trait above all others that makes a person unhappy, frustrated, and unable to cope with life's surprises. That one trait is the compulsive need for control. We all have some wish to control the things around us. Those of us who have wrestled with this need in ourselves probably know how difficult it is to stay open to learning when what we really want to do is change that situation or that other person to conform to our wishes.

Unfortunately, no matter how good we get at controlling things or other people, we never feel very much in control because we are looking in the wrong place to get this need met. We try to control the things that happen to us instead of looking at how we react to the things that happen. We are enacting Security/Control values in what is fast becoming a Learning/Discovery world.

Franklin was a powerful man—fast-talking, physically strong, and temperamentally unbending. He ran his large, highly profitable construction company like a well-oiled machine. Workers were expected to do their jobs efficiently and without questioning the time-honored ways of doing things. If employees did dare to suggest alternatives, they were subject to rebuke. He felt that this management style was effective because profits were up in a down market.

There was only one problem with Franklin's organization: turnover was over 50 percent per year. Fewer than half his employees remained with him even a full year.

He was not the type of man to ask for help with his problems, but his brother-in-law, whom he respected, persuaded him to hire a management consultant to evaluate his organization's effectiveness. When the consultant talked with Franklin about possible reasons for the high turnover, Franklin was at a loss to explain this fact.

As he and the consultant developed a relationship over the next few months, trust began to grow between these two men. Franklin was able to use Ted, the consultant, as a sounding board for his "off-the-wall ideas."

In time, he began expressing to Ted some of his self-doubts about his management style—doubts he had never shared with anyone, including his wife.

As these coaching conversations continued, Franklin became more and more open about his personal pain. He revealed to Ted that he was addicted to amphetamines, that without them he felt tired, irritable, and depressed. So he had no choice, he felt, but to medicate himself.

This confession, while offered in part as an excuse for his irritability, turned out to be the beginning of the end of Franklin's denial that his life was not working and neither was his company. Sure, he had enough money to keep "throwing at his company's problems," but money only served to mask the fact that his way of managing his life and his organization was not sustainable.

Admitting a problem of this magnitude was not easy for a proud man like Franklin. He had to trust that Ted would not be judgmental or moralistic. It was Ted's style to simply mirror back to Franklin just what he saw and what he was hearing from his client —like a video machine playing back a tape. Eventually, Franklin was able to see himself clearly, without distortion.

He realized, "I have been feeling out of control of this company for years. I built this company to where it is all by myself, and no one but me seems to care about it. I guess I held on too tightly somewhere along the way. . . . I think that's why no one but me cares. And now all I have is my title and my money and the external symbols of power."

Spurred on by this realization, Franklin began a course of self-study and self-change. He joined a recovery program to help him kick his drug habit. He took some leadership development courses recommended by Ted. He got into marriage counseling with his wife after realizing that she, too, was getting tired of being dominated. And, with Ted's help, he began to meet regularly with employees to listen to their ideas about how to make the company a healthier, more productive environment.

A year later, profits had doubled and turnover had dropped to 5 percent. But more important, Franklin was feeling in charge of his life. "It's remarkable," he disclosed. "I'm asking for help from perfect strangers. I'm sharing leadership for the company with people who have only been here six months. I'm letting my wife win some of the time. . . . And I've never felt more powerful in my life!"

Often, when people like Franklin feel out of control of their lives, they resort to substitute gratifications such as drugs, alcohol, cigarettes, food, sex, work, or other people. These substitutes meet the "pseudo need" to do something that will have a predictable result—that is, to get a feeling of being in control. In our effort to fend off unwanted feelings, these substitutes distort our perception and mask the deeper need that hungers to be satisfied.

This deeper need is to feel connected to ourselves and in control of our inner state. We long to feel peaceful, happy, self-accepting, and related to others. We need to trust that whatever happens, we will be able to cope with it. Failing this, we seek substitutes to help us feel the security that we long for. To the degree that we mask our unhappiness through such escapes, we weaken our ability to receive accurate feedback from our surroundings. We are training ourselves in the dangerous art of denial.

Franklin's relationship with Ted gave him an objective, accepting mirror, which enabled him to break free of his denial, face himself honestly, and learn what his life crisis was calling him to learn.

As the stress in our world increases, the human tendency to engage in denial and self-deception is on the rise. When we lose our ability to feel real pain and to hang out with discomfort long enough to figure out what to do, we're in trouble. We make impulsive decisions. We reach for quick fixes in our attempt to escape the discomfort of not knowing. Instead, we must learn to tolerate ambiguity and discomfort and to search longer and harder for answers in places, and from people, we never would have thought to investigate.

Franklin attempted to stay in control through using stimulants and through punishing employees who didn't "color within the lines." When he finally opened up to learning and let go of his compulsive need for control, he began to face the real problem and grow beyond it.

The Payoffs of Learning/Discovery

In the Learning/Discovery attitude, you gain a sense of control not from making people do what you want or from making things come out right. Your feelings of personal power come from your state of mind, from an inner attitude that allows you to maintain your sense of balance no matter what disappointments, shocks, or crises come your way. Learning/Discovery is the ability to live in a continual state of openness to being surprised. When we are focused on learning, as opposed to controlling, our attention naturally goes toward discovering what the current situation requires of us. We do not consume valuable time and energy wishing things were different or trying to control other people. Neither do we indulge our fantasies about how things ought to be. We accept the world as it is and get on with doing the best we can with what we have.

With the Learning/Discovery mind-set, we have a built-in centering mechanism that allows us to feel okay no matter what the outcome. When things go well, we celebrate. When they don't, we learn the appropriate lessons. Either way, we can't lose! We maintain our center, our sense of well-being, regardless of whether things turn out as predicted. Others recognize this quality of inner calmness, and people are more apt to trust us, want to affiliate with us, and do a good job for us.

People are becoming conscious of the fact that you can't run away from the problems life deals you. When you do, don't you often find yourself facing the same problem again in your next job, your next marriage, or your next neighborhood? You can't run away from yourself. Wherever you go, there you are! If, instead of running, you face up to the problem and learn to deal with it, this sort of thing no longer presents a problem for you. This is what it means to make yourself while making a living.

The Essential Differences

The essence of Learning/Discovery is an openness to learning from everything that happens to you, especially the disappointments and mistakes. Learning/Discovery takes a relatively objective view of what is. It has few expectations. And it does not take unwanted surprises personally.

The essence of Security/Control is a fear of things turning out wrong. Thus, there is an attempt to manipulate, control, or maneuver situations to be "the way they are supposed to be." Your ability to make a living is threatened if you encounter unwanted surprises. In this mode, there are definite expectations of how things should go. When things do not go as planned, someone is in trouble.

This chart summarizes these two contrasting sets of assumptions. You will see at a glance how the two approaches differ with regard to the six strategic meta-skills introduced in Chapter One.

Security/Control as Compared with Learning/Discovery

Security/Control Approach	Learning/Discovery Approach

Resists Change
  Sees change as disruptive.
	Participates with Change
	  Sees change as natural.

Holds On
  Holds on to what was or what should be.
	Lets Go
	  Lets go into what is.

Focuses on Externals
  Values appearance over essence.
	Focuses on Essentials
	  Values inner essence over appearance.

Communicates for Control	Communicates to Build Trust
Attempts to get others to agree.	Wishes to know and be known.
Thinks in "Either/Or" Terms	Thinks "Both/And"
Uses polarized, black and white thinking.	Looks for mutuality and complementarity.
Fosters Poor Teamwork	Fosters Team Learning
Cannot share responsibility and power.	Shares responsibility and power.

In Learning/Discovery, you are open to being changed by the significant experiences of your life. This helps you anticipate changes, cope with potential crises, and adapt creatively to circumstances that are beyond your control.

Charlotte was the CEO of a twenty-person public relations company. She was having trouble getting along with her vice president for finance, Stephen. She was extremely sensitive to Stephen's frequent moodiness. When she perceived that he was upset or irritated, she would try to avoid him; but this created two problems: she would end up doing some of his work for him so she didn't have to bother him; and she would waste a lot of energy (although she hated to admit it) worrying about what she might have done to provoke Stephen.

As I worked with Charlotte, Stephen, and the rest of the top team to clarify their vision, mission, and values, I modeled the Learning/Discovery attitude. Every time Stephen showed his characteristic upset when things did not go his way, I would look at my own reaction, such as a tendency to want to treat him with kid gloves, and comment on the fact that I was noticing this tendency in myself. I did not blame Stephen, and I did not try to get him to change, although I'll admit that at first I had quite a bit more empathy for Charlotte than for Stephen. I truly did see my reaction to Stephen as a problem for me to handle, not as something that he was responsible for. As the others saw me learning and growing in my ability to hold my own with Stephen, they, too, got into the spirit of learning new people skills rather than trying to change Stephen.

After a few weeks, Charlotte told me she had experienced a

profound transformation in her attitude toward Stephen and toward the other annoyances in her job: "I just realized that my job here is one big personal growth experience. I can't control what happens, but I can always learn from it. Now that I'm viewing life this way, the things that used to bother me don't bother me anymore. Even when Stephen seems to be manipulating me with his moods, I just step back and ask myself, 'What's the best way to handle this?' And then I handle it. I've stopped thinking that he should change to make my life easier. And strangely enough, everything feels easier now." Charlotte got her first lesson in making herself participate in change, and in so doing found new enthusiasm for making a living.

In the Security/Control mode, people attempt to protect themselves from pain, disappointment, failure, bad news. This can lead to defensive distortions in perceiving or interpreting current reality. In one company I consulted with, the CEO would get hurt feelings if someone pointed out to her a better way of doing things. She would act insulted and then snub this person in public for several weeks afterward. Pretty soon, people stopped giving her their good ideas. Obviously, a company cannot afford this sort of blockage in the information flow.

To make good decisions in today's complex world, we need more knowledge more quickly from more sources than ever before. This requires teamwork. Everyone seems to favor teamwork these days, but becoming a team learner requires a willingness to *learn in public*—something that most people find difficult. Learning in public means you are able to admit to your teammates when you don't know something that you may think you should know— so you can get needed help from others. It means you are able to publicly acknowledge mistakes, when this would serve the team's learning. It means you are able to share your perceptions with your group (or partner), even if you think you are the only one who feels this way.

To be a team learner, you need to place more value on the team's learning than on your own personal needs to be right, to be accepted, or to feel in control. Learning/Discovery fosters the ability to listen and learn from people who see things differently than you do. This is a vital component of team learning. Healthy conflict produces innovative solutions. When we can respectfully differ from others in public, without judgment or blame, we are creating a context where team learning can occur.

Managers, supervisors, and the rest of us, too, need to listen and learn from each person's contribution. We need to help every single person feel that his or her resources are vitally needed. When workers feel connected to the organization in this way, they tend to become leaders also, participating as full partners in helping the organization live up to its potential and meet its goals. Teamwork becomes a tangible reality, not an abstract ideal.

Learning/Discovery is not a fad. It's here to stay. It is not a new belief system, but a way of continually updating and modifying our self-perceptions, paradigms, assumptions, and beliefs. It is not even a learning system. It is a posture of openness to whatever happens. There is a paradoxical sort of stability in committing to a life of continual learning and change. We can relax, knowing one thing for sure—nothing's forever, nothing's for sure.

CHAPTER THREE

Assessing Your Learning/ Discovery Potential

In times of shifting paradigms, we tend to operate with a foot in both worlds. In certain situations, we may be pretty controlling. At other times, we can be amazingly open to learning.

The goal of the chapter is to help you recognize when you are operating out of your need for Security/Control and when you are coming from the Learning/Discovery mind-set—when your intent is to control and when it is to learn.

As you do these various self-assessment activities, see if you can maintain an attitude of exploration and discovery. Try not to get caught by the Security/Control part of the mind that will want to portray a desirable self-image. You will learn more by expressing yourself genuinely than "correctly." And if you do find yourself pulled back to the Security/Control attitude, you can use this as an opportunity to look again at the defenses your mind uses to protect itself from feeling out of control. That awareness is an important step in learning to stay more and more in the Learning/Discovery mind set. You really can use everything, even this, to learn about yourself.

Meta-Skill Builder 1: Scenes from a Workplace: A Self-Assessment

This section includes descriptions of typical workplace scenarios. While reading each one, notice your gut reaction as you imagine yourself in this situation. Then ask, "How would I handle this?" and select the option closest to how you think you would actually behave. When you get to the end of this section, we will score and discuss your answers.

Scene 1. You notice that your supervisor has seemed preoccupied every time you go to her office to speak with her. You have an urgent need that concerns a deadline you know is important to her. The last three times you have tried to get her attention, she has given you a gesture that seemed to be saying, "Not now; come back later." What do you do?

A. Keep trying in the same manner you have been.
B. Give up, saying to yourself, "It's her problem if this thing doesn't get completed on time."
C. Nonverbally indicate to her the urgency of your need. When you get her attention, ask her if she will have a brief discussion with you about it.
D. Write her a note that both explains your agenda and respects her need to deal with it later. Ask her if she will give you a few minutes to discuss it—and if so, when would be a good time.

Scene 2. You are George's supervisor. On Monday you ask him to proofread and edit a report you have prepared for senior management. You ask him if he can get it back to you by the end of the day. He says that he can. As the day goes by, you notice George at his desk working on your report. He comes out every hour or so for a cup of coffee, says nothing to anyone, and goes back to his editing of the report. At the end of the day, he drops the copy of the report on your desk. You thank him. He grunts without looking at you and leaves to go home for the day. When you look at the report, you see red scribbles splattered liberally over the entire first three pages. The last eight pages are untouched. The editing that he has done seems overly critical in places. In other places, his remarks just don't make sense to you. What do you do?

A. Ignore the whole thing. Act as if it never happened.
B. Compliment George the next time you see him on the helpfulness of his comments.

C. Invite him to meet with you the next day to discuss the reasons for his editorial comments. At that time, tell him you have always respected his work, but felt that this time the reasons for his comments were unclear to you. Ask him if there is something going on for him or between the two of you that you aren't aware of.

D. Go to him the next day and say, "George, I can't understand where you were coming from when you marked up my report. Your comments didn't make any sense at all. And you never even got to the last eight pages. What were you doing with it all day?"

Scene 3. One day your boss calls you into the office with what seems to be a friendlier-than-usual attitude. After you have been seated, he says with a big smile, "I have an opportunity for you! Have you heard of the Cerido Institute? Well, they offer employee development programs—programs where you can learn how to better manage your time and your stress. We have money budgeted for two of our people to go to their week-long training program, December 15 to 22. I'm strongly recommending to Personnel that you be one of those two from this company. (Pause) I feel it is important to your job that you go. How about it?"

A. You ask with a smile, "Am I being *sent?*" You assume he feels there is something wrong with the way you manage time and stress.

B. You ask why he has chosen you, what he sees about your performance that makes him feel you would benefit from the program. You don't assume anything. Then you ask if you can take some time to talk the decision over with your family.

C. You tell him you'd be happy to attend. You assume he sees this as an honor, a reward for a job well done.

D. You ask if you can take some time to talk the decision over with your family. You assume there is pressure on you to attend, that it will cost you at performance review time if you don't go. Still you remain firm in your need to make your own decision independent of the consequences to your job.

Scene 4. It is time for you to give semiannual performance reviews to the six people who report to you. One of these people, Thomas, is performing somewhat below par, but more significant is his attitude. Thomas does all jobs to the minimum of your expectations. He seems never to expend much effort or energy. At the appointed hour, Thomas comes into your office, looking somewhat sullen. He sits down. How do you open the meeting with Thomas?

A. "Thomas, I don't feel we know each other as well as I'd like. I think I'm always a bit too busy to really get to know what people need in the way of support and resources. Do you feel supported enough around here?"

B. "Thomas, if you don't give this job more effort, we're going to have to put you on probationary status."

C. "Thomas, do you like working here?"

D. "Thomas, I'm going to begin by asking you how things are going around here for you, what you feel good about and not so good about. Then, I'd like to have you rate yourself along our ten review criteria. After that, I'll give you my feedback. How does that sound?"

Scene 5. You and your supervisor seem to have very different styles of working. She keeps a lot of projects going on all at once, does everything very rapidly, and tends to make many errors as a result. You prefer to do things more slowly and thoroughly.

Today she calls you in to ask you to do something: "This time I'll only ask you to do half of what I usually ask of you, because you seem to be under a lot of stress. The jobs I'm expecting you to complete before our next team meeting are —, — and —." You believe that each of these three jobs could easily take the full time allotted for the three. And besides, you have other work that you are in the middle of completing. How do you respond?

A. You tell her what you are currently working on and ask which, if any, of these things can be put aside for a while so you can work on these projects. You then ask her how thoroughly she expects the three jobs to be done. You tell her that it is your style to do things more slowly and carefully and ask if this style creates any problems for her.

B. You tell her that you are already overloaded with work and aren't sure when you will get to these three jobs. You mention some problems you are having with a coworker and a problem you are having at home, both of which are slowing down your efficiency.

C. You agree that you are under great stress and ask what she knows about filing a stress disability claim.

D. You tell her you appreciate how quickly she seems to get things done and ask her if she has any tips for you. You acknowledge that your natural pace is more slow and careful. You ask if your style creates any problems for her. You then tell her that you are concerned about doing a good job by your own standards while at the same time meeting the deadlines she has to work with.

Scene 6. You have just finished an important piece of work, one that you feel may affect the future of your career. Although you feel you did a good job, you're not sure how your supervisor will evaluate it. In the past, your supervisor has not been a person to offer feedback very easily. Thus, you have a hard time knowing where you stand. Just as you are thinking these thoughts, your supervisor comes to your office and asks, "Well, is it done yet?" How do you respond?

A. "Yes, here it is."

B. "Yes, and after you have had a chance to look it over, could you let me know what you think of it?"

C. "Yes, and after you have had a chance to look it over, I'd like you to tell me whether you see any potential problems with the design, and whether the methodology conforms to the criteria that the board has set forth."

D. "Yes, and after you have had a chance to look it over, could you give me some feedback—either in writing or in person, whichever you prefer."

Scene 7. You are the principal in a high school of approximately four thousand students. Your school's campus contains a main building where most academic classes are held, and two outlying buildings where art and music classes meet. This morning, Mr.

Bradlock, one of the art teachers, informs you that there is no heat in the two outer buildings. You check with the head of maintenance, and he tells you it may take several days to do the needed repairs on the heating system. Since it is a very cold day, you feel that this situation must be dealt with at once. You consider moving all art and music classes to the library, and asking the teachers who usually take their classes to the library for research to remain in their regular classrooms today. You also consider asking Mr. Bradlock and the other art and music teachers what ideas they have. What do you decide to do?

A. You take matters into your own hands because you want to be perceived as supportive of your staff. You inform the academic faculty that they may not use the library until the heating problem is cleared up in the outer buildings. You inform the art and music staffs that they should now move their teaching materials and equipment into the library until heat is restored in their facility.

B. You inform Mr. Bradlock and the other art and music teachers that it may take several days for heat to be restored in their areas. You invite them to meet with you to brainstorm options for dealing with the problem, assuring them that you will support whatever decision they agree on.

Scene 8. You are manager of a twelve-person department that will soon be reduced in size because of budget cutbacks. You have been told that your budget has been cut in half and that you will therefore have to lay off six employees within three months. How do you handle your communications with your department?

A. You begin watching very carefully the six people you expect to let go in order to document why you chose to cut out their jobs and not the others. Two weeks before their severance date, you inform them individually that you are giving them two weeks' notice (the minimum time required by law in your industry).

B. You sit down with each individual in your group and tell him or her that some jobs will need to be cut over the next three months. You explore with each their long- and short-term career goals, options for possible reassignment or early retire-

ment, and any other options they see for themselves. A week
later, you have a meeting where people can share ideas and
feelings about the issue. You encourage honest expression of
feelings. You also facilitate a group problem-solving session
where people are invited to brainstorm ideas for keeping each
person employed at the level he or she wants.

C. You announce at a department meeting that your group will be
reduced in size. You give people a chance to ask questions. You
tell them that you do not yet know who will be leaving and who
will be staying.

D. You go immediately to the six people you intend to terminate
and ask if they have any other employment options. You make
your decision regarding who will stay and who will leave based
on your assessment of who could best handle being laid off.

Scene 9. You are regional sales manager for a large publisher of
educational materials. Your company has just been bought out by
an even larger company, one whose corporate culture is stiffer, less
friendly, and more structured than your home company. You now
report to the vice president for marketing and sales from the other
company. She invites you in to discuss a plan she has for combining
several departments from her company and several from your company and placing them all under your management. What do you
think when she proposes this? What do you say?

A. You have serious doubts about the advisability of doing this all
at once. You would like to see the transition managed a bit more
gradually and with more dialogue and participation between the
two groups about what sort of new structure would serve the
mission of the new company. You mention that you have reservations, but since she doesn't ask what they are, you don't elaborate.

B. You have the same feelings about her plan as in item A above,
but in this case, even though she doesn't draw out your reservations, you ask her if she'd be willing to listen to them. When she
tells you to go ahead, you outline your concerns.

C. You do everything you did in choice B above except that before
you tell her your thoughts, you draw out from her why she is
suggesting the immediate combining of the three departments.

You listen attentively and respectfully. You let her know that you see her point. Then you offer your ideas in a language and tone that emphasizes how your plan will solve the problems she is trying to solve with her plan. You ask for her feedback on your idea, and listen carefully to her objections.

Scene 10. You are an upper-level manager for one of the nation's leading car-manufacturing companies. Because of foreign competition, your company is faced with the need to quickly develop a new product that it does not really have the engineering, data processing, or manufacturing capabilities to support. Adding this new product would mean doing a rush job done in a haphazard way. You envision the enormous additional resources the company would need, and you do not feel the company should try to keep up with the competition in this case. You know this new product would be your manager's turf. You also know that you would be the one to implement the change. What do you tell your manager?

A. You do not wait to be asked for your opinion. As soon as you get word of the proposed change, you speak to your boss about your assessment of the situation.

B. As soon as you get word of the proposed change, you ask to have a meeting with your boss. You ask questions about the rationale for the new product launch, focusing especially on ascertaining where your boss's self-interest lies. You listen attentively and respectfully. You open your mind to her view, and you let her know that you see her point. Then you offer your concerns, honestly but without extraneous emotional undertones. You are not attached to her buying in to your objections, but you do everything in your power to present a calm, well-reasoned case.

C. You do what is asked of you and keep your concerns to yourself. You think to yourself, "What if I'm wrong about my assessment? I'd better not say anything."

How Did You Do?

Now let's look at your responses to these scenes. Remember you are evaluating your answers based on the following criteria:

- What was your intent—to control or to learn?
- Were you open to the other's views? Did you seek to know and be known?
- Were you hiding your real feelings out of fear or the need to put forth a certain image?
- Did you show respect for your differences?
- Did you "fill in the blanks" when you didn't know something (by leaving assumptions untested, for example), or did you ask for the information you needed?
- Was there anything in your style or tone that indicated the intent to control or manipulate the other? Was there perhaps an intent to control that you were not aware of at first?
- Did your answer try to control the other's response by hiding the truth, playing it safe (so as not to risk anything), not rocking the boat?

In **Scene 1,** you are receiving nonverbal signals not to interrupt your supervisor. This happens several times in a row.

If you answered A to this situation, you are doing what most people would probably do. But you know the old saying, "If you do what you've always done, you'll get what you've always gotten." This is a Security/Control response. You did not do anything to show a desire to learn from the situation. You may be operating out of a fear of confronting your supervisor, *assuming* that this will displease her. Remember to watch out for the tendency to assume instead of checking out your hunches. You may be having trouble envisioning how to break in on someone without being perceived as rude or engendering criticism. In the Security/Control mode, people go to great lengths to avoid criticism or looking bad.

Answer B is also a Security/Control response. Again there is nothing in your behavior that would indicate an intent to learn. Perhaps you do not wish to rock the boat, or you may be assuming that she realizes that your question is related to her deadline. Both of these attitudes, playing it safe, and assuming rather than asking, tend to be associated with the need to feel or appear in control.

If your C answer comes from a sincere desire to learn from and about her, it is a Learning/Discovery response. If it is done in a pushy way, coming from the wish to control, it is Security/Control. If it is Learning/Discovery motivated, you are taking the risk of displeasing her in an attempt to know and be known. You have some important data that she needs in order to make an informed decision.

Answer D clearly represents the Learning/Discovery mode. In D, you give information in a way that allows her complete freedom to respond or not. You are fully respecting her autonomy, while at the same time asserting yourself fully—a Both/And response. You give weight to both your own and the other person's reality. The Learning/Discovery attitude thrives on information and strives to accommodate both your needs and the other's.

Scene 2 was the situation where George edited your report in a way that did not make sense to you.

If you answered A, this is a Security/Control way of handling things: *No news is good news. If I don't know about it, I don't have to take responsibility for it.* Unfortunately, this is a rather shortsighted attitude. George is communicating something important to you by his actions. The only trouble is, you have no idea what he is trying to say. You may be sweeping a conflict under the carpet, leaving lumps of debris that you'll have to clean up later on in your relationship.

Answer B could also lead to future problems because now you are not only withholding your true reaction from George, you are giving him positive feedback that could reinforce his unclear communication. This is a Security/Control response.

In answer C, you are approaching the problem from a Learning/Discovery attitude. You don't jump to conclusions. You wait for him to tell you about his reasoning. You seek information with genuine curiosity, and you give information to let him know your feelings about what he did. Your curiosity helps George feel you are interested in him. Your openness to learning about his needs and feelings builds trust. You revealed some of your own vulnerability, which helps him feel safe to be honest with you. You create a climate of safety before you confront him with your feelings. In the Learning/Discovery framework, honesty is a high value. And honesty is a two-way proposition. Whether people are honest with you depends partly on the attitude with which you approach them.

Answer D is Security/Control and would decrease your chances of getting an honest, nondefensive response. In D, you launch right into your complaints before establishing contact, before building rapport, before letting him know that you respect him and value your relationship with him. Most people would respond to the D approach in a defensive manner.

Scene 3 has your manager offering you an opportunity to attend a weeklong time-management training session just before Christmas.

In A, you are *assuming* that he is being critical of your performance. This is a Security/Control response. Assuming we know something when we do not is related to the need for control. It reveals a need to have all the answers, to avoid the experience of uncertainty or ambiguity.

Answer B is a Learning/Discovery response. You don't assume. You ask for information in an open, nondefensive way. In some cases, it is okay not to give any information about your own position until you have heard the other's reasoning.

Answer C may be entirely truthful, but there is no opportunity for learning. It jumps to the conclusion that this is a reward, thus depriving you of an opportunity for some useful feedback about your performance. Thus, it is a Security/Control response.

Answer D keeps you in control all the way. You are indicating to him that no matter what he wants, you will make your decision without input from him. This is a Security/Control response because it is so unilateral and because it, too, is based partly on an assumption about his motives that you have not checked out.

In **Scene 4** you are having a performance review meeting with Thomas, a do-the-minimum type of guy.

If you answered A or D, you are doing business in the Learning/ Discovery mode. Answer D asks questions that yield more information. Even though your question in answer A was of the yes-no type, it does more to build rapport because it exhibits caring. It is thus likely to elicit a fuller response from Thomas.

Answer B destroys whatever rapport you may have with Thomas by immediately taking a posture that is adversarial rather than supportive. When you set this sort of tone, the other person usually follows your lead, especially if you are in the leadership position.

Answer C, a Security/Control response, seeks only a yes-no answer which, given Thomas's performance to date, may not yield much information and may leave you both rather unsatisfied.

In **Scene 5** your supervisor has asked you to do too much work in too little time.

Answers A and D are Learning/Discovery responses. You give information about your needs. You ask for information about hers. And you ask for some specific, relevant feedback. In addition, in answer D, you build rapport by showing genuine appreciation and interest before getting into substantive issues that might surface your differences.

Answer B is an attempt to get what you want (control) via playing up your weaknesses. People who manipulate with weakness are pretty transparent to most supervisors. With this approach, you may get what you want in the short term, but it will not further your sense of mastery or control over your own destiny.

Answer C is a thinly disguised threat or manipulation, something that people often resort to when they feel pushed to do something they don't want to do. This creates an adversarial interchange and destroys the opportunity for mutual problem-solving.

Scene 6 finds you wondering where you stand in terms of your performance.

Answer A is a Security/Control play-it-safe response. You play the part of the model employee, but you are still unsure how your supervisor sees you.

Answers B, C, and D all indicate Learning/Discovery thinking. Answer B asks for feedback in an attitude of genuine curiosity. Answer C tells your supervisor more specifically what type of feedback you'd like. And answer D not only says what you want, it also tells him how you would like him to deliver it. Answer D may be preferable for a supervisor who has a hard time giving feedback because it offers him options that he may not have considered.

In **Scene 7** you are a school principal confronted with a breakdown in your school's heating system.

Answer A may appear to be a supportive and efficient response to such a crisis. However, most employees would prefer to be consulted before being moved from their usual work space. The one-way, noncollaborative nature of answer A puts it in the Security/Control category.

Answer B is the Learning/Discovery response to this dilemma. You trust the collaborative problem-solving process rather than taking control and solving the problem in a way that makes sense to you alone (as you did in answer A). The B answer allows for the possibility that there may be factors that only the teachers are aware of. It opens you to learning about others' ideas and feelings. It's a bit messier, but may lead to a better solution because people are more supportive of decisions that they have participated in making.

In **Scene 8** you are dealing with a proposed reduction in force.

An A answer is Security/Control. It reveals an attempt to cover your bases by documenting any instances of substandard performance from the six employees you plan to let go. Documentation would not necessarily indicate Security/Control thinking in and of itself; but the fact that you already know before you collect the data whom you are going to fire is the critical factor here in defining answer A as Security/Control. It is insincere. Also, the fact that you waited until the last minute minimizes the opportunity for two-way communication. This cuts down on the opportunity for mutual learning.

Answer is B Learning/Discovery. You both give and receive information. You are interested in looking at alternative ways to deal with the predicament rather than just the one obvious way. You are showing yourself to be open to experimentation and innovation.

Answer C is again Security/Control. You do give people the chance to ask questions, but there is no intent to learn. Your intent is to keep control of the situation. You do not encourage real dialogue on the issue. You do not show an interest in the others' feelings and ideas. You appear reluctant to deal with the full complexity of the situation.

Answer D is a Security/Control response. You do seek information and engage employees in a somewhat controlled dialogue. But it appears as if your decision will be based on the need to avoid painful feelings, not necessarily on what will be best for the company and all concerned. If a dialogue is used to give the illusion of openness, but the intent is still to control, it is not a Learning/Discovery response.

In **Scene 9** you find yourself in the midst of a merger. You could choose between A, B, and C, all of which are Learning/Discovery. Option A has fewer L/D elements, option B somewhat more, and option C the most. In option C you not only have a Learning/

Discovery plan for dealing with the merger, you are willing to listen respectfully to her plan, and you gear your response to her concerns. The C response embraces more points of view and more different bits of information. It offers the possibility that the people involved can learn something from each other.

In **Scene 10** your company wants you to get involved with a new product that you don't believe in.

Answers A and C are Security/Control responses. In A you seem to expect that your voice is going to have more impact than it probably will have, given the fact that you did not give your new boss a chance to explain her concerns. We need to listen to others if we expect them to listen to us. The Learning/Discovery stance takes account of this principle. In C you seem to be withholding information to avoid drawing attention to yourself. This is the don't-make-waves-no-news-is-good-news-bury-your-head-in-the-sand-it's-not-my-problem attitude. These familiar attitudes are all examples of the Security/Control mind-set.

Answer B shows a Learning/Discovery orientation. You consider your manager's position with an open mind without giving up your own viewpoint. You show genuine curiosity. You value both the information you are receiving and the information you are giving. You trust yourself to handle the uncertainty and ambiguity that accompanies genuine two-way dialogue.

Now that you have looked at a variety of real-life situations from both the Security/Control and the Learning/Discovery perspectives, which fits more naturally with your personal style? If you tend toward the Security/Control end of the spectrum, there are good reasons for this. Maybe you were not aware of the alternative. Or perhaps you feel that style just fits you better because of who you are or where you have been. Or maybe you have been working to let go of some of your control needs for some time with only limited success.

Meta-Skill Builder 2:
Mapping Your Need for Control

Let's look at where you are now, your present situation, with respect to these two ways of being in the world. Take out a sheet of paper, and on the far left side of the page, make some notes or draw a picture characterizing your present need for control. It could be high, medium, or low. Just represent it in some way on paper. Now at the far right side of the page, make notes about, or draw, where you would like to be. Then, in the middle of the page, note the stumbling blocks that you think might be blocking you from getting where you want to be. Blocks could be things like fear of retaliation if you tell it like it is, reluctance to look weak, or discomfort with conflict. Noting the stumbling blocks can help you target where your efforts need to be in making the shift toward Learning/Discovery.

It's not good to push yourself to change if you have not dealt with your fears and resistances. There are reasons for these fears that cannot be denied or overpowered. You need to listen to your resistances to hear what needs they are serving—like protection— for example. Then you need to look for other ways of providing that same sense of safety while you work to lessen your need for protection. Only then will you be able to let go of your resistances to change.

Now note all the advantages you can think of about being where you presently are, things like "It feels like me," "It gives me a feeling of knowing what I'm doing," "People notice and look up to me." Once you have listed the benefits of being the way you presently are, see if you can think of any other ways to get the same result. For example, if you said "People notice and look up to me when I take control," are there other ways you might get noticed or recognized? Perhaps you could get a similar result by remaining calm and centered under fire or by showing genuine curiosity toward other peoples' views.

In Part Two, you will learn about the six meta-skills that will help you make the transition to the more flexible and open Learning/ Discovery attitude.

Developing
YOUR
CAPACITY
for
LEARNING/
DISCOVERY:
Six Strategic Meta-Skills

Participate with the Change Process

If we understand that life itself is an ever-changing process, then we will feel connected to change rather than alienated from it. We will be able to sense the subtle winds of change and act accordingly rather than getting caught in a hurricane. This is what it means to participate with the change process. You feel at one with change. You feel yourself continually shedding the old to make room for the new.

Embracing Learning/Discovery means you come to identify yourself as continuously changing, always in flux. This can be somewhat disconcerting at first. But that's the essence of Learning/Discovery —you eventually get used to being part of a constant flow that is greater than yourself. You expand your sense of identity to include your participation in the rhythms and cycles of life.

The better we understand the rhythms and cycles of change, the more fully and powerfully we can participate with them. Toward that end, I would like to offer you a map that describes the stages in a typical change process. Having such a map of change reminds us that even though change is unpredictable, there are some familiar landmarks to watch for. Knowing these landmarks helps us find our way when we feel lost or stuck. It gives a sense of order and meaning to an otherwise chaotic situation. It shows us what's likely to come up next, so we can prepare for it or even help it happen more easily.

In this chapter, I will describe the eight stages that most of us go through when we encounter the need for change. To give you a feel for how you might actually experience these stages, I'll start by describing how two of my former clients, Derek and Jenny, dealt with important changes in their lives.

Derek

Derek was forty-eight when his wife Helene informed him suddenly that she had filed for divorce. The couple had two teenage daughters. Although he and Helene had drifted apart somewhat over the past few years, he thought they had a good marriage. He had no idea that she had been so unhappy. The news sent him into a state of depression.

At the time, he was manager of a twelve-person data-processing department in a *Fortune* 100 company. As far as he knew, everything at work was going fine—except for the fact that he didn't get along very well with his manager.

The crisis in his marriage caused Derek to take a closer look at his life. He had always seen himself as strong, confident, and in control. Now he felt weak, vulnerable, and unsure of himself. After suffering alone with these feelings for several weeks, he decided to take advantage of his company's employee assistance program. The EAP counselor set him up with another, longer-term counselor, so that he could look more deeply into how he had gotten into this predicament and where he wanted to go now.

The first thing Derek realized was that he had been in a state of denial for most of his life. His marriage had never been satisfying for him, but it was secure, and he had become dependent on his wife. When he looked honestly at his relationships at work, he saw that they, too, were in need of repair. His performance evaluations had been less and less favorable over the past few years. He felt misunderstood by his manager, but had not dared to look at what he might be doing to contribute to this misunderstanding. He began to suspect that his sense of himself had always been pretty shaky. Now that he was in counseling where it was okay to show vulnerability, he saw that he had built his self-image upon his ability to get other people to do what he wanted. This included his wife, his daughters, and the people who reported to him. He was now able to make some sense of his wife's complaints that he always had to have things his way, and of his manager's feedback that people found him overcontrolling and unresponsive.

He came to recognize that his rigid personality was a compensation for his massive self-doubts. He was trying to appear in control because he felt so inadequate most of the time. He could see this wasn't working anymore. Even his daughters, who had always been "Daddy's little girls," were pulling away. He could sense their criticalness, and this hurt him deeply. He feared growing old all by himself with no one to care for him.

As he and his counselor reviewed his life story to uncover the roots of his self-doubts, he recalled that his father had abandoned him and his mother when he was nine years old. At that point, he felt it was his job to be the man of the house and take care of his mother. So he suppressed his own pain and insecurity in favor of becoming "the little man." He was still a little boy, of course, so he had to pretend that he knew what he was doing. If anyone differed with him, he couldn't handle it because he had not yet developed the resourcefulness of a mature man. He lacked confidence in his ability to deal with the unexpected, so he demanded that others conform to his wishes and plans. This rigidity was what his manager and coworkers found difficult to work with.

He told his counselor that he had attended numerous management-training seminars on how to coach and empower others, but these approaches seemed unrealistic and impractical. His counselor helped him see that he was critical of this newer management philosophy because adopting it would demand that he develop better interpersonal skills and more tolerance for ambiguity than he was comfortable with. This newer philosophy was like a foreign language. He knew how to give feedback to his staff, but he never put himself in a position to receive it from others.

Over the course of the year following his wife's departure, he got to know himself a lot better. He allowed himself to feel unsure and self-doubting, and was surprised to find that he was not devastated by seeing these things in himself. He went through several months of not knowing who he was anymore. He sought out advice from the people he supervised, and found that he could handle difficult feedback and even use it to make himself into a better manager.

His depression gradually lifted, and his interest in life was renewed. He even felt some gratitude to his ex-wife for being the catalyst for these changes. Now that his hope was restored, he began to think about how he would like his life to be. He envisioned himself as an empowering person instead of someone who has to dominate every situation. He thought about what kind of lifestyle he wanted, and decided that he would like to develop a good relationship with himself before attempting another relationship with a woman. He decided he would begin to listen more to his daughters, instead of lecturing them. This was his picture of how he wanted to be.

During the two years that followed this revisioning of his life, Derek's company ran into financial troubles. Top management decided to eliminate over 80 percent of their middle-management positions, replacing these with self-managing teams and a more streamlined organizational structure. While Derek's performance evaluations had improved significantly over the past two years due to his personal changes, his job was still in jeopardy. Many of his fellow managers were in a panic, but he remained relatively calm. As soon as he heard of the proposed changes, he began to gather information to help him realistically assess his options. He talked to his manager about the possibility of remaining in his present post —even though he had a sense that a change of bosses would be good for him. He interviewed upper managers in other departments in the company, both at his current location and in other parts of the country, to see about transfer possibilities. He considered a variety of options: staying at this location versus relocating, remaining in management versus returning to computer-programming, staying with his present employer versus seeking employment elsewhere. All of these questions were considered in light of his vision of himself as a more empowering, empathic person.

He decided that he wanted to stay in management, but that it would be okay if he had to relocate to another branch of his present company. He also knew that if this was not possible, he still had other options. In a few months, he was offered a management post at another location of the same company. He accepted it, and after a year in that position, he now finds that the changes he envisioned for himself have been hastened by the job change. "It gave me a chance to start over. I could be the way I wanted to be instead of the way I had always been," he disclosed.

Shortly before moving to his new job, he met a woman who had also been going through her own personal change process. He decided that he wanted this relationship to be one where there was a commitment to open, two-way communication—where he would seek her input and feedback instead of ruling the roost. They were married recently, and now he is having a chance to do marriage differently. His new wife has two sons in high school, so he is also getting an opportunity to parent in a new way. He loves his job in a way that he has never felt before, so now balancing his love for his family and his love for his work takes some attention. He has realized the vision he had for himself and is moving on to new challenges.

Jenny

Jenny was manager for a group of engineers in a large high-tech company. An engineer herself, she always considered herself more of a "techie" than a people person. Since becoming a manager two years ago, however, she found herself spending most of her time in meetings, both formal and happenstance. It was very difficult to keep people from taking up too much of her time in matters she felt were not her job. She found it difficult to establish and communicate her "boundaries," to set limits on how much help she would give or to say no to people who needed something from her. This meant that she spent many nights at the office trying to finish up her work. Her husband and young son were upset by her long hours, but Jenny felt caught in the middle between a job that she basically liked but which had gotten out of control, and her family, whom she knew she was neglecting. Jenny felt "overworked and underloved," as she put it. This was not a sustainable state of affairs.

Unlike Derek, Jenny did not wait to be knocked down by a crisis. She could sense that something was not right with her life. She felt pain over the fact that she and her husband had not had a real conversation in months. She could see herself overeating instead of nourishing herself in more appropriate ways. She realized that she had a habit of denying the importance of her own needs and feelings, that she had the dangerous tendency to allow herself to be walked on by others. She also had the inner strength to face her situation and say "This is going to change." But for a while, she didn't see much that she could do differently. She needed to sit for quite a while with the "this has to change" feeling before a vision of what to do could emerge.

As she took stock of her life, she saw how easy it had always been for her to take care of other people instead of asserting her own needs and opinions. She had grown up in a household where her father dominated, and her mother adapted. Now she was allowing her job to dominate her while she tried to adapt to its every demand.

Fortunately, Jenny knew that she was good at what she did. She had some fears, however, about the reactions of her manager and employees if she started to stand up and set limits. Her manager was a people-pleaser himself and often found it hard to do anything that might hurt anyone's feelings. Jenny knew she would have to make the personal changes she envisioned without much support from him. The picture Jenny saw of her future self in her mind's eye was one of calm, compassionate firmness. She envisioned herself answering peoples' questions succinctly without overexplaining. She saw herself listening openly to her employees' complaints without accepting these as excuses for poor performance. She imagined herself refusing to argue with a certain hot-tempered coworker, but instead suggesting that the two of them reconvene when he was ready to deal with her more respectfully.

The process she went through to get from where she was to where she wanted to be consisted mainly of honest self-observation. Summoning the courage to admit she had a problem was the biggest hurdle. Then she began to watch herself in action, without judgment or blame. She saw how often she withheld the truth from people in order to protect their feelings and avoid a hassle. She saw how easily she was drawn into solving problems that did not belong to her. This honest self-appraisal, combined with frequent discussions with her husband about what she was seeing, led to profound changes in Jenny's approach to management. Each time she saw herself behaving in a way that did not serve her goals, she would "Monday-morning-quarterback" the situation, envisioning a better way to handle it. She would then experiment with new ways of dealing with these situations when they recurred.

While she received no verbal praise or encouragement from her manager, she could sense his respect for the changes she was making. Occasionally, she would go to him and report her handling of a difficult situation, both to educate him about what he should now expect of her and to give him the information he needed to support her if her actions happened to be questioned by someone else.

Jenny's change process, while relatively quick, was not without its periods of fear and self-doubt. She felt fear whenever she approached an old situation in a new way. She felt fear before going to talk with her boss about handling a situation in a way that was more formal and businesslike than perhaps he would handle it. She allowed her fears of change to coexist alongside her wish for change. She knew this was normal—that fear is a signal that we are moving into unknown territory, not a signal to turn back.

Jenny is still changing and growing. She is pleased with how far she has come in so short a time. When that hot-tempered employee began a tirade of insults in her direction, she felt proud of how she handled it. Displeased with something she said to him in a meeting, he stormed into her office after the meeting was over. She calmly told him that she was not open to discussing the matter in this tone but that she would be happy to sit down with him tomorrow and talk about it. She reassured him that she was open to his views, but that she could not accept disrespectful behavior from him or anyone else. He came in the following day, calmer and more collected, and they had a productive discussion about the incident.

Jenny's home life is happier, too. The spark is back in her marriage. Her son no longer feels like he is getting only her leftovers. And she has started a regular program of physical exercise to replace the "nourishment" she was getting from overeating.

The stories of Derek and Jenny illustrate how two people navigated the typical storms of change. Both had to overcome very strong habits of denial in order to gain the courage to face themselves honestly. Both still feel great sadness about the time lost to them because of those years of denial. From where I sit, as witness to their journeys, I know that in time their sadness will lessen—because they both have a lot of life ahead of them, and in the years ahead they are not likely to go back to living with their heads in the sand.

As you reflect on the stories of Derek and Jenny, do you notice any parallels between their lives and yours? When have you felt that something needed to change in your life? Have you ever denied that change was called for? When you have set a new course for yourself, what storms or floating debris have you encountered on your voyage? What has helped you stay on course or get back on course? How do you feel now, in retrospect, about the changes you have weathered or chosen? And most importantly, what have you learned about yourself in the process?

If we review what Derek and Jenny went through in their change processes, you will see eight somewhat distinct yet overlapping stages:

Stage 1: Feeling Unsettled. *Something isn't right.* (Derek and his wife were not communicating; his performance evaluations had been getting less favorable each year. Jenny felt "overworked and underloved.") These feelings may be denied, and thus unconscious, but they influence your sense of happiness and self-esteem. They also cause noticeable incongruence between your words and your actions.

Stage 2: Denying/Resisting. *It's really not that bad. Maybe I don't have to let go of my familiar way of doing things.* (Derek told himself that he had a "basically good marriage." Jenny denied the seriousness of her situation for a long time before waking up. She had been completely unaware of how unhappy she really was.) Often the first two stages alternate in the dim recesses of your awareness before emerging into consciousness.

Stage 3: Facing the Present Situation. *I see things as they are.* (Derek saw how rigid his behavior was and how this was affecting his relationships at home and at work. Jenny saw herself spending too much time at work, eating too much, and neglecting her family.) You have the courage to admit how bad things have gotten, without dramatizing or exaggerating. You also take note of the resources you presently have for creating positive change.

Stage 4: Letting Go into the Unknown. *The ways of the past are not working, but the future is still unclear.* (Derek admitted that he did not know the language of empowerment. He wasn't sure he could learn a whole new way of being. Jenny knew she needed to be more assertive, but wasn't sure how to do this. She spent a lot of time just observing herself to discover who she was and what she wanted.) You mourn the loss of the familiar old ways. You surrender to the uncomfortable feeling that you don't know what to do, and perhaps don't even know what you want.

Stage 5: Envisioning the Desired Future. *I know what I want.* (Derek decided he wanted to stay in management, but with a more empowering style; and that he wanted to develop a good relationship with himself before getting involved with a woman. Jenny envisioned herself setting limits and asserting her needs calmly and firmly.) Clarity about your wants and goals begins to emerge out of the haze.

Stage 6: Exploring the New Options. *Maybe I can do it.* (Derek interviewed higher-level managers in several locations. Jenny observed herself doing things in her characteristic style and then Monday-morning-quarterbacked her behavior.) You try on various new ways of being—both in your mind and in actuality.

Stage 7: Committing to Action. *I can do it.* (Derek decided to take a new job with more responsibility. He began a new relationship based on two-way communication and mutual learning. Jenny told her manager about the changes he could expect from her. She talked about her change goals with her husband as well.) You create the necessary structures in your life that will allow the "new you" to be expressed.

Stage 8: Integrating the Change. *I am doing it.* (Derek is now enjoying his work more than he ever has in his life. He has discovered a new relationship to his work. As this change occurs, he now faces the challenge of balancing the demands of work and family life. Jenny is dealing with people in the firm, compassionate manner she envisioned for herself. She no longer worries about hurting others' feelings. Her manager is supportive. Her family is delighted.) You find a new relationship to those aspects of your life that were causing pain. You do not eliminate them, but rather you relate to them with more of yourself present.

Obviously, no "map" such as the one above can do justice to the complexities of real life. Still, letting go of the old does lead to something new. You are not destined to be in limbo (the letting-go stage) forever, even if it seems like forever while you're in it.

Real change is not just doing something else, like changing jobs or marriage partners. Real change, real learning, involves discovering new or formerly hidden dimensions of your personality and then integrating this new discovery with what you already know about yourself. As you learn and grow, you keep bringing more of yourself to the party. When you embrace Learning/Discovery, life becomes an ongoing process of "making yourself."

Meta-Skill Builder 3:
Assessing Your Openness to Change

Think of a situation in your personal or professional life where you felt something wasn't right and did something proactive. Describe the situation: who was involved; the setting; your feelings and fears; the constraints that you felt; what you felt you might gain and lose by taking action; how you made the decision to do what you did; what you did; the outcome; how you felt afterward; how long it took you to integrate the change; how you feel now in retrospect; what you learned about yourself through this process.

Now think of a situation where you felt something wasn't right and did nothing. Again, describe the situation: who was involved; the setting; your feelings and fears; the constraints; what you felt you might gain and lose by taking action; how you made the decision; the outcome; how you felt afterward; how you feel now; what you learned.

As I present these stages in greater detail below, think of the two change situations you have just reviewed in your mind, the one where you took action and the one where you did not. Note how your change process parallels the eight stages, identifying where the process went smoothly and where you had difficulty.

While many of the changes you go through in your life will be triggered by outside events rather than your own feeling that "something isn't right," if you learn to participate with the change process in dealing with the changes you choose, you will be much better prepared to deal creatively with those imposed by forces outside your control.

Stage 1: Feeling Unsettled

This stage is characterized by such feelings as "Something isn't right," "I'm not able to get what I want with my present resources," "I feel dissatisfied with the way things are," "This situation does not bring out the best in me," "I'm not sure what to do."

The Eight Stages of Change
stage
task of each stage
skills needed at each stage
what you need to let go of to develop through the stage
what you learn from completing each stage

	Stage 1: Feeling Unsettled	Stage 2: Denying/Resisting	Stage 3: Facing the Present Situation
TASK:	allow myself to feel unsettled; admit dissatisfaction	recognize my resistance or denial for what it is	face my situation realistically; see what it is
SKILLS:	ability to feel unpleasant feelings	ability to overcome or manage my fears	nonjudgmental, nonblaming attitude
LET GO:	my attachment to always feeling fine or in control	my denial or resistance	old picture of who I am or how things should be
LEARN:	I can handle pain/discomfort.	I understand how my denial/resistance is an attempt to protect myself.	I can move ahead into the unknown without triggering more denial/resistance.

The Eight Stages of Change (cont.)
stage
task of each stage
skills needed at each stage
what you need to let go of to develop through the stage
what you learn from completing each stage

	Stage 4: Letting Go into the Unknown	Stage 5: Envisioning the Desired Future	Stage 6: Exploring New Options
TASK:	grieve the losses associated with saying goodbye, including what I lost by hanging on too long to an inappropriate situation	visualize what I want or how I want to be in the future	exploration of the new options I have envisioned for myself; experimenting with new behaviors and feelings
SKILLS:	ability to feel sadness, ability to tolerate uncertainty	ability to feel wants	ability to take risks
LET GO:	the need to know what I want and where I'm going	safety of sticking with what is familiar	having to be good at everything I do
LEARN:	I can handle not knowing where I'm headed or how things will turn out.	I trust that something new and more appropriate emerges out of the chaos.	I am open to new ways of being and doing things.

	Stage 7: Committing to Action	Stage 8: Integrating the Change
TASK:	commit to action; choose the option(s) that seem most appropriate	integrating the new quality/ behavior into the rest of my life; bringing more of my whole self to the party so that I operate at a higher level of complexity and maturity
SKILLS:	ability to make decisions and eliminate options	ability to allow my various traits and impulses to communicate with one another; ability to feel and act on more than one impulse at once in an integrated way
LET GO:	other alternatives; the need to keep all options open	the sense of loss associated with choosing this instead of that; the need to have the perfect answer
LEARN:	I can envision something new and make it a reality.	I can continue to learn and grow.

Sometimes there is simply a vague sense of boredom or discontent. Other times the pain is acute.

To most people, feeling unsettled is not a good feeling. Some of us were taught early on that to be upset meant there was something wrong with us, that we were somehow wrong or bad. Perhaps we grew up in families where weakness and dependence on others were frowned upon. When you feel unhappy, upset, or in need of comforting, your first reaction is to tell yourself, "Everything's gonna be alright," and move immediately into denial as a defense against feeling "bad" feelings.

This is a typical reaction, given the norms of the American culture. We are a can-do society. To admit that we can't or don't know what to do doesn't fit our self-image.

Rather than feeling "I don't like what's going on here," or "I'm afraid of making a mistake or looking foolish," people in this can-do culture of ours tell themselves, "Everything is going to be fine," or, "It's so terrible that nothing can be done about it." These defense strategies keep us doing, feeling, and thinking what we have always done, felt, and thought.

The Stage 1 awareness that something isn't right often alternates with Stage 2 denial that there is a problem. Your feelings may shift back and forth between feeling dissatisfied and telling yourself it isn't that bad or things will get better soon.

The task of Stage 1 is to admit to feeling unsettled, to allow the "Something's not right" feeling into consciousness. This sets the change process in motion. To be open to learning, you must have the capacity to feel discomfort without blaming or judging yourself as wrong for having this feeling. You need to let go of the belief that if you don't feel good, that means you are somehow wrong or bad.

In order to do this, you first need to address your fears or resistances to feeling pain or upset. You may have habits or fears that protect you from emotional discomfort but which get in the way of perceiving things as they are. You cannot change until you discover more appropriate ways to maintain your sense of safety.

Thus, if you bolster your sense of competence by denying your need for help, you will have to find another way to feel competent before you can let go of your denial. Perhaps you will need to include within your definition of competence the fact that you have a commitment to continuous improvement and learning, and such learning is served best by being open to help from others. To let go of your resistance (in this case your denial of the need for help), you must first acknowledge your outdated belief and then find another more up-to-date belief that will serve you better.

Facing and accepting the present situation as it is, without blame, guilt, judgment, or whitewashing—this is the primary skill needed to navigate through this first stage of change. If you can't feel, you can't feel unsettled. And if your self-image says you're always in control, you can't let yourself feel unsettled.

Think back to the situation you identified in Meta-Skill Builder 3, on page 68, where you felt the need for change and did something about it. What triggered your feeling that something wasn't right? Was it an emotional event, a political or social event, a physical feeling in your body, a comment or observation by someone you care about or respect? How long did you go on feeling this way before you felt yourself begin to move through the other stages of the change process?

Stage 2: Denying/Resisting

This stage is characterized by such self-protective statements as: "Everything's going to be okay," and "Maybe if I ignore the problem, it will go away." We each have our favorite ways of avoiding uncomfortable feelings.

Have you ever known anyone who was unexpectedly fired from a job or divorced by a mate? When I talk to my friends who have had these experiences, they report that they knew for quite a while somewhere deep inside themselves that something wasn't right; but they tried to defend themselves against the painful awareness —usually through denial or false hope, or through trying to manipulate the situation. Essentially, denial means lying to yourself; and manipulation means getting someone else to lie to you. Either way, you are ill prepared to anticipate coming changes.

Again, recall a situation in your life where you did nothing even though you knew a change was called for. What did you tell yourself to help ward off the sense that something needed to change? You may recognize in yourself one of these familiar forms of denial:

"It'll get better if I can be more patient." "There's nothing I can do about it." "This is not really hurting me that much." "If it's happening to me, I must have caused it, and therefore it's my lot in life—I must deserve it." Or perhaps you can see yourself more easily in these blaming responses: "If you hadn't set such a stringent deadline, I could have succeeded." "If only you would trust me, I wouldn't make so many mistakes."

These defensive strategies help us feel comfortable and in control, but they interfere with our ability to perceive the present situation as it is. We need to overcome our tendency to protect ourselves from discomfort if we want to stay in touch with the feedback available to us. The need to appear in control inhibits our ability to take appropriate action and to learn what we need to learn.

Since the impulse to deny or resist change often alternates with feeling the need for change, it is important to allow these two feelings to coexist side by side within your conscious awareness, rather than pushing one impulse out of your awareness. When you can feel your mixed feelings, your push-pull, it is only a matter of time before the truth will emerge. Often the way out of denial is by admitting that a big part of you is afraid of the loss associated with change or simply doesn't want to change. Acknowledging this paves the way for facing the situation squarely.

Stage 3: Facing the Present Situation

This stage is characterized by feelings such as "I admit I need help," "Now I see what I should have done," "I can no longer escape the facts."

Once you have seen and accepted your initial resistance to admitting the need for change, you can see the present situation as it is, without blame or judgment.

In changing her management style, Jenny was helped to face her present situation by naming her unhappy state, "overworked and underloved." Giving a name or a descriptive phrase to what you are experiencing can help you keep the reality of it in focus. There is sometimes a tendency to go two steps forward and one step back in this change dance. Naming the situation helps you keep from going backward.

As you face the fact that change is needed or change is occurring, you may also feel some grieving taking place. Even as you look forward to something new, and possibly more desirable, you may feel some pulls backward to the things you will miss. If you gloss over these feelings, you will miss important information about yourself. Moving into the unknown can be both scary and exciting. Leaving the familiar can be both a relief and a loss. These mixed feelings may be confusing at first, but allowing them to coexist can help you integrate the changes taking place.

It helps to actually sit down and make a list of all the things about the present situation that you will miss, and all the things you would like to be rid of. Imagine yourself without these things in your life. Feel the loss of these things. Then feel the relief about the things you're glad to be finished with.

Facing the present situation involves both fear and wish, both trepidation and excitement. By the time you have completed this stage, you will have had lots of practice in holding within you simultaneously two seemingly contradictory feelings. This ability to contain discrepancies develops your inner resilience. You are becoming more change-worthy—more able to take change in stride.

Meta-Skill Builder 4: The Gap Exercise

There is a useful goal clarification exercise that can help you stay on course at this stage. It is called the "gap exercise" because it asks you to focus on where you are now, where you would like to be and on the gap between where you are and where you would like to be. I introduced a briefer version of this exercise at the end of Chapter Three (Meta-Skill Builder 2 page 55).

You'll need a large piece of paper. In one corner, draw a symbolic image of your present situation, indicating how you feel now. For example, if you feel overwhelmed, you might draw yourself in the middle of an ocean with a giant wave approaching.

Then, on the opposite corner of the page, depict where you

would ideally like to be—maybe on a sunny, freshly mowed golf course.

Next draw an imaginary route from here to there, complete with stepping-stones and stumbling blocks. You might want to label some parts of your picture, identifying specific resources you can draw on to help you attain your desired state. You might also wish to label some of the pitfalls you know to watch out for. The gap exercise gives you an overview of your present situation. It helps you see the whole of your current reality.

Stage 4: Letting Go into the Unknown

This stage is characterized by the feeling "I'm lost; I don't know where I am or where I'm going." It's like being in limbo—sailing off into uncharted waters with no land in sight. This can provoke anxiety.

Your old familiar ways don't feel right anymore, but you do not have any new and better ways either. You are waiting to see what is next for you.

There was some comfort in your old ways, however, and there may be things you will miss. At this stage, it is important to take note of what you are letting go of and grieve for what you will no longer have. It's a good idea to name these things specifically, and create a ritual in which you say goodbye to them.

The best way to approach this stage is with an open, humble, ready-to-receive-instructions attitude. You may notice a tendency in yourself to escape the discomfort of not knowing by engaging in compulsive activity or busyness. Do not rush to fill in the blanks with answers. If you can, allow yourself to feel "I don't know what to do; all I know is how I feel from moment to moment." And pay attention to your various feelings, thoughts, and intuitions. These will eventually form themselves into a coherent picture of what you want and what you need to do. Appreciate your efforts to stay with the anxiety rather than rushing to "fill in the blanks."

Think of a question you have about your life for which you do not have an answer. Perhaps there has been a situation or event that has occurred, and you don't understand why it happened.

Allow yourself to be puzzled over this event. Formulate a question about the event in your mind. Sit with this question without trying to come up with an answer. Perhaps an answer will come in time as you continue to hold the question. But do not *try* to get it resolved. Just get used to being in a state of not-knowing. It's good practice. You'll get better at this with time.

Stage 5: Envisioning the Desired Future

This stage is characterized by such feelings and thoughts as "This is how I'd like my life to be"; "When I have achieved my goal, I'll be able to . . . , and I'll be more . . ."; "Right now I'm . . . When I get where I'm going, I'll be . . ."

Your vision is the result you want to achieve. It is good to create a specific, clear, tangible image of how you want your life to be. Jenny used the appealing phrase "calm, clear, compassionate" to focus her energy on her desired future. In other instances, your vision will emerge from the fog without your doing anything to construct it.

The ability to envision what you want helps you to be proactive about change. Change is much easier when it is voluntary.

Visioning has become a very popular tool in recent years for helping people and organizations to attain their goals. If you want your vision to really work, the vision should fulfill the following criteria:

1. *It must be realistic.* It must take into account your actual needs, resources, and the limitations of the system you are in (yourself, your family, your organization).

2. *It must be inclusive.* It must be arrived at in a way that includes or takes account of all parts of the system. Ideally, all parts of the system (including all parts of yourself) would have a voice in creating the vision. If this is not feasible, at least allow all parts to offer comment or input.

3. *It must be specific.* It must include specific descriptions of how to get there and how you will know when you have arrived.

4. *It must be transformative.* It must represent real learning, not just a behavior modification. For example, if your vision is to

be fit and healthy, you must do more than eat less and exercise more. You would need to transform your relationship to food and exercise.

5. *It must be held lightly, without attachment.* You may encounter new information that could cause you to reevaluate or revise your goals. Remember that the new, revised vision may be more appropriate than the older one.

A clear and well-articulated vision can reduce the amount of effort, waste, and conflict in a system. When you have your aim always in mind, you can assess your every action and decision according to whether it serves your aim. You will be more confident and decisive as a result.

A scientist for Genentech, Inc. described to me how his company uses visioning to eliminate the need for job descriptions and lengthy work assignment meetings. Every Monday morning, teams meet to review team and company vision and mission. This is followed by a general discussion of how to turn the vision into a reality. Workers then go back to their jobs with an overall sense of what needs to be done and where they fit into this picture. They do what is needed without ever being given a specific assignment.

The following Monday they all come back together to review what each has done. Without task assignments from management, the group finds that each scientist or engineer has carried out his or her piece of the overall vision in a coordinated, synergistic way. The Monday meetings align the workers around the group goal. This promotes a high degree of efficiency, cooperation, and harmony.

Stage 6: Exploring the New Options

This stage is characterized by the attitudes "If I do this versus that, what will I gain and lose?" and "So this is how it would feel if I chose that."

In this stage, you do a lot of trial and error, both hypothetically and in real time, in order to discover which options are most realistic and most expressive of your vision. You are testing the waters to see if you are really ready to jump in.

Derek visited other divisions of his company in other locations.

Jenny tried out being more assertive first with a supportive co-worker before doing so with the more difficult ones.

This is also the time to play out various "If/Then" scenarios: If I do this, what are the consequences likely to be? If that happens, are there other, perhaps unexpected, consequences that could result? If/Then scenario-building allows you to look for the untoward side effects or fallout that might result from a change.

As you get clearer on what you want, more energy is focused on the future and less on the past. You are letting go of your resistances gradually, in stages. You may know where you want to go, but you're not sure how to get there. Or you may not even be sure where you want to go. This is the stage where you do something even if you are not sure you are doing the right thing. You accept that life is a trial-and-error process. You try something you think will be effective. Then you see if it works. If it does, good. If it doesn't, you have learned something.

If you have tendencies toward perfectionism, your fear of doing the wrong thing may come up at this stage. In Security/Control, we often worry too much about doing the wrong thing. We waste time worrying and ruminating when we could be experimenting and learning something. We put off making a decision until we have more data. The only problem with this attitude is that all the really important decisions must be made without sufficient data. Being willing to let yourself be wrong in order to discover what's right is an important decision-making skill. People who cannot let go of control and the need to look good cannot do this. They become paralyzed, overwhelmed by their need to consider all the facts before acting. Nowadays there are just too many facts. It is not humanly possible to consider all of them.

Go back again to the situation you identified on page 74, where you felt a change was needed and did something. Did you do any exploring of options as part of your change process? If so, was it useful? What did you learn from your exploration? If nothing, why not? Were you afraid of anything? If you could do this stage over, would you do anything differently?

Stage 7: Committing to Action

This stage is characterized by such feelings as "This feels right," "This is what I have been working toward."

During the previous six stages, a process of alignment has been gradually taking place. The process of arriving at a readiness to commit is similar to what happens when a group reaches consensus. The various parts of your personality tug and pull you in different directions. Eventually you feel "of one mind."

A group or an organization cannot move forward in one clear direction until differences in values and approaches have been resolved. Likewise, you as an individual cannot commit to anything as long as you are at war within yourself.

The commitment stage occurs after you have acknowledged and worked through your fears and resistances and after you have explored some of your options. If you believe you are ready for committed action, and things still aren't working, this could mean that you need to go back to one of the earlier stages and complete something. Often in such cases we find some resistance that was overlooked, suppressed, or not fully dealt with. There was a voice that we did not listen to in our rush for closure.

Recall an action you took that was arrived at after some deliberation. Can you identify any of the elements of your ambivalence? Were some of your values or feelings pulling you in one direction, while others were pulling you in the opposite direction? Did you attempt to suppress or overpower either set of feelings? If so, how?

In the research study I did for the book *The Couple's Journey,* I found that couples go through years of struggle and resistance to their differences before finally settling in to the "Commitment Stage." This stage is characterized by their ability to act in unity. This ability is only developed after couples have learned how to accept their differences and use these differences for mutual learning and creativity. People and organizations tend to be impatient with the time it takes to achieve consensus, but unless differences have been opened up and dealt with, no true commitment is possible.

Getting to this stage requires getting our different impulses and feelings into communication, and eventually into alignment, with one another. No commitment is possible until all the various parts in a system (your organization, your marriage, your personality) are in good communication with each other. (Chapter Eight, "Cultivate Both/And Thinking," includes additional tools for bring disparate parts of a system into harmony.)

Stage 8: Integrating the Change

This stage is characterized by the feeling "I can relax; I have finally come home." You have learned new, more satisfying ways of being or doing things, and these new ways now feel like they belong to you. Your new ways make you feel as if you have become more of who you really are.

You have let go of certain outdated habits, fears, or beliefs, and are now identified with the new—for as long as that lasts! You have new skills to support your deeper, more inclusive identity. Now you need to create a support system in your environment to help you maintain what you have gained. If you make personal changes that are not supported by your environment (organizational culture, mate's values, etc.), it will be difficult to sustain the change.

Creating a support system involves identifying people who accept and value the change you have made. Perhaps they have been through something similar in their own lives. To sustain the change, you need to be around other people who share your commitment to ongoing learning. It is not very supportive to be around people who only accept you if you conform to their way of being or doing things. Your support network should be composed of people who will be there after the next major change in your life as well.

If you do not have such a support system, the first step in creating one is to admit that you need one. Then keep your attention open to finding the type of people who will be supportive of your learning. An openness to receive on your part will help you attract what you need. This is one of those mysterious laws of how things come into being. (Chapter Ten, "Joining Forces with Your Organization," offers additional tips on how to develop an ongoing support system for learning and discovery.)

Meta-Skill Builder 5: Making It Happen

Think about a change that is needed in your workplace—something where the need is openly recognized by others and where you have some leverage or influence. Map out the situation using the gap exercise discussed on page 75. Then imagine yourself guiding the change through all eight stages. Note the changes you might undergo personally as you guide this process. Are you willing to be changed? Are you willing to learn something about yourself during the process of facilitating change for your organization? If you are, you will engender trust for yourself and trust for the process of change. If you are not, do not be surprised if you encounter more than the normal amount of resistance. People can sense it when you are passing off a job that you yourself are unable to handle. In the new workplace, who we are speaks more loudly than what we say.

How Participating with Change Can Make You Indispensable to Your Organization or Your Customers

1. Being a participant with change means that you define yourself as continuously developing and refining your abilities. When your prime motive is to seek new ways to add value, this attitude is going to be noticed and appreciated by others. And once you set the tone with this attitude, it is likely to be contagious because people have a natural drive to grow in their ability to make a contribution.

2. The best way to build trusting relationships with others is to show them that you are open to learning from them. When you understand and participate with change, you see learning as a natural part of your daily routine. Here are some things you might do in the normal course of your day:

Ask your immediate supervisor to assess your ability to facilitate and lead change as part of a performance discussion. Ask about things you could do to help make her job easier.

Ask the people who work for you, or with you, to give you feedback on how they see you dealing with and/or leading change.

What do you do that is helpful? What could you do differently or better? If there are aspects of their feedback that you do not understand, ask questions and stay in conversation until you do. Do not explain or defend yourself. Thank them for their contribution to your learning.

Ask a valued customer for ideas about what your function should be doing in your organization. Then discuss how this is similar and different from what you think. Jointly agree upon and carry out a plan that involves using some of this customer's ideas.

Create a self-improvement support group with a group of co-workers. Meet regularly to brainstorm ideas about how each of you could improve your personal effectiveness. Then do the same for ideas about improving each person's functional area in the organization. Award prizes for best ideas and for most ideas implemented.

3. When you understand and trust the change process, and can embrace change in your own life, you are then equipped to lead others in change. The new workplace needs more people who can assume leadership regardless of their formal job duties.

How Participating with Change Can Help You Prevent or Respond to Crisis

It is probable that in a very few years, the present structure of jobs and the way work gets done will look entirely different than it does today. To participate successfully with such radical societal changes, it is important to be well versed in the art of feeling, sensing, and seeing the signs of change in advance of a crisis. It behooves you to make it your daily practice to actively notice what is not working in our present system, without judgment or blame, and to become interested and engaged with this phenomenon.

And Remember:

- Admitting that "something isn't right" is the most important step in the entire change process. This sets into motion the other seven stages of change.
- Resistance is a normal part of the change equation. Admit that a

big part of you (or your organization or group) does not want to feel that things are not right. Step up to meet your fears and resistances rather than denying or suppressing them.

- Aim for solutions that account for the complexity of the situation —that address the potential side effects or "fallout" of the proposed action. Beware of simply rearranging the deck chairs on a sinking ship.

CHAPTER FIVE

Let Go and Go On

One of the biggest blocks to learning is holding on to perceptions, attitudes, and beliefs that no longer serve us. If we are to stay in touch with current reality, we need to constantly let go of the fantasies, fears, and automatic habit patterns that keep us from experiencing the present moment.

If you wish to solve problems before they become disasters, you need to know when to let go. Learning involves letting go of a version of the truth that no longer serves you in order that a new version may take its place. Deep personal learning requires that you let go of the ways you shield yourself from feeling insecure and out of control. Often it means letting go of what you already know or what you think should be happening, so you can see what really is happening. This could mean letting go of the need to be right, to look good, or to know the right answer. Or it could mean letting go of anger, resentment, guilt, or shame about something in your past or letting go of worry about your future. To let go is to surrender to what is happening, to let yourself fully experience your present situation so that the natural change process can do its work.

Let's consider the predicament you might be in if you had just discovered that you made a rather costly mistake. Do you own up to your error as soon as you recognize it? Or do you wait, hoping that time will erase its impact? Mistakes in the new workplace are often quite time-sensitive. Sometimes, letting go quickly and asking for help can spell the difference between success and disaster.

Roberta was vice president of marketing for a major airline when her company learned that the competition were all introducing frequent-flyer programs to boost sales. The president asked her to be in charge of implementing a similar program for their company: "I know it'll be a tough job, but if anybody can pull it off, you can. You've done the impossible so many times before." Roberta felt honored to take on the challenge. She had a reputation for being a can-do type of person and liked being so highly regarded by the company president. As she began researching her task, however, she discovered that if the program were going to work, the company would need a much more sophisticated computer system. As it turned out, there were no resources available to implement such a system, so she would have to make do on a shoestring.

Over the course of a two-year period, Roberta attempted to put the program together without the proper infrastructure. Not only did she lack the technical resources to do the job, she did not have an adequately trained staff.

She worked brutally long hours, did the whole program on an outdated computer system with people she had to train from scratch. The stress from overworking became so serious that she began to lose her hair. Her husband resented the extra time she was spending at work and asked for a separation. When the program was finally in place, she was divorced and wore a wig. And if these personal failures weren't enough, the program itself limped along for six months and eventually folded.

In retrospect, Roberta confides to me that her intuition told her all along that she was attempting the impossible. She was unable to admit that the job could not be done with the available resources. She held the unrealistic belief that if it didn't get done, this was a personal failure. She had a reputation to maintain as a superstar. She could not allow herself to admit the possibility that she could not do the job assigned to her. This did not fit her self-image. And besides, the president had put his faith in her.

So instead of letting go and accepting the situation as it was, she held on to her picture of how it should be. "In the end," she lamented, "my inability to admit that the situation was beyond my control cost me my health, my marriage, and my reputation."

As a postscript to this story, shortly after the project failed, the company president realized that he needed to commit more resources to the job. He installed the required computer system, hired a team of specialists from outside the company, and the program was successfully implemented within three months. Roberta got no credit for her efforts. In fact, she was seen as wasting the company's resources when she should have known when to give up.

Why was it so difficult for Roberta to let go? Perhaps a clue to the answer lies in her unexamined belief that letting go is a *defeat*. What a strange irony—in trying to hold on to her image as a winner, she wound up failing miserably. If she had acknowledged the reality of her situation, instead of pretending to be up to an impossible job, she might have come out a winner.

In Chapter One, I introduced the idea that crises occur to call our attention to something we need to learn. If we apply this idea to Roberta, what was she being asked to learn?

While there were probably many things to be learned from her situation, she clearly needed to learn to let go of her need to be seen as always in control. She needed to release herself from this attachment to how things should be, so she could deal with the actual conditions of her predicament.

This may mean accepting that she is not superwoman, that sometimes she needs help in order to succeed. Knowing Roberta as I do, I know how reluctant she is to let go of her supercompetent image, even when it sabotages her success. She sees it as a personal failure when she has to admit that she cannot do something. She thinks that asking for help equals weakness.

She did not see how this belief was preventing her from dealing realistically with her situation. If she had, she could have examined the origins of this belief and reevaluated it in light of present circumstances. Often, we operate according to rigid personality patterns founded upon unexamined assumptions and beliefs.

In Roberta's case, she had a tendency to automatically say yes to anything anyone asked of her. This grew out of a belief learned in childhood that to be worthy of esteem you must do what you are told without question. Under the conditions of her current work situation, this belief was no longer useful. But since she was not aware of it, she could not reevaluate it and let it go. (In Chapter Six, "Focus on Essentials," we will consider in depth how to identify and move beyond self-limiting beliefs.)

Once again, we see the importance of letting ourselves feel unpleasant feelings. They may contain the information we need to make the decision to let go. The attempt to avoid such feelings keeps us out of touch with current reality and unable to change and learn.

How do we learn to feel more okay about unwanted feelings—so we can access the information they offer? Too often, if something makes us hurt, we assume it isn't good for us, and we avoid it. But as Roberta's story shows, *only by letting go into an unpleasant truth can we be saved from it.*

The first stage in the eight stages of change involves the capacity to feel "something isn't right." This feeling can occur in an instant, as when a squall comes up unexpectedly at sea. Or it may take months or years to develop, as it often does when we are first getting signals that some familiar habit or behavior pattern is no longer serving us. When such a feeling creeps into awareness, it is important to look for what we are being asked to learn or let go of. In our overly positive, can-do culture, we often steamroll right over our discomfort in an attempt to get back to feeling in control. We have come to associate discomfort with being wrong, bad, or inadequate.

When we learn to include *feeling uncomfortable* within our definition of *being in control,* we greatly expand our ability to cope with change and crisis. We do not waste energy resisting discomfort. We more accurately perceive when change is called for. We do not need our defensive patterns of denial and manipulation. We accept disappointment instead of seeking someone to blame. We do not hold on to minor mistakes or insults from others, thus freeing our attention for creative response to the present moment.

We have all had difficulty letting go at some time in our lives. If you have gone through a divorce, for instance, you can probably remember the pain of loss, uncertainty about the future, and doubts about yourself.

Those of us who have gone through the divorcing process know that with time we do let go and often with a sense that we have benefited from going through the pain. Surprisingly, the same is usually true for the loss of one's job. It may be traumatic while we're going through it, but later on most people realize some meaning in it all.

Why can't we remember these things when we are in the midst of some seemingly catastrophic change? Why do we so often make things worse for ourselves by fighting the inevitable? It is our resistance to change at work here. It is so much easier to see what we are losing (because we just had it) than what we are gaining (because we have not seen that yet). Our resistance is our attempt to protect ourselves from pain or loss. But this strategy usually backfires, and we wind up suffering (like Roberta) more than if we had surrendered.

The real art of letting go is the ability to let go of ways of being, seeing, and doing that no longer work—letting go of what was or how things were supposed to happen to make room for what is happening: letting go of our outdated self-picture so we can see ourselves as we are now; letting go of our disappointment and anger so we can forgive and begin again; letting go of dwelling on some recent mistake or foolish remark so our attention is free to deal with the effects of that mistake or remark; letting go of worrying about what someone else might be thinking of us so we can base our self-concept on our own actual feelings about ourselves.

Learning to Let Go

Life is full of unwanted surprises: our own mistakes, disappointments, or betrayals by others, reversals of fortune, acts of God. When we are faced with an unwanted surprise, we often cannot get beyond our resistance. Change can be painful in a variety of ways. We may feel awkward, ashamed, angry, vulnerable, helpless, resentful, uncertain, or afraid.

Just remember those are growing pains you are experiencing. It will hurt a lot less if you don't resist. On the other hand, people do resist the pain of growth and healing—so we need to deal compassionately with our fears and resistances.

Resistance, while it is a nuisance on one level because it may weaken our ability to perceive the need for change, is useful on another level. We need to know what our fears are so we can confront these fears, understand their source, and do what's necessary to get reassurance or support so we can go on. Resistance is information about what we need to learn, let go of, or heal.

How do we practice the art of letting go? In the remainder of this chapter, we will look at the six most common ways we block learning by inappropriately holding on. In each section, we will also consider how to learn to let go.

Ways we block learning by holding on:

1. Holding on to a self-perception or habit that no longer serves us
2. Fear of the past repeating itself
3. Fixating our attention on things we have no control over
4. Avoiding our feelings through addictive or compulsive habits
5. Suppressing our feelings
6. Trying to control other people

1. Old Self-Perceptions and Habits

There is an old joke that illustrates the difficulty we have letting go of familiar ways of being. A woman drags her husband to see a psychiatrist. "My husband thinks he's a chicken," she tells the doctor. "Tell him he's not a chicken; he's a man," advises the psychiatrist. Her reply: "I would, but we need the eggs." It's hard to let go of old habits. There are secondary gains, or "eggs," associated with any familiar way of being. Your eggs might be the fact that this habit protects you from the risks of success—risks like responsibility, visibility, or authority. Or, like the husband in the joke, other people may be depending on your staying just as you are. If you change, they have something to lose.

Meta-Skill Builder 6:
What Are You Holding On To?

Let's examine whether you are holding on to something because of the "eggs" it provides for you or someone else. Take a slow, deep breath, and as you do so, allow your mind to scan your present situation. Look at each area of your life in turn: your work, your family, your health, your possessions, your friendships, your avocations and interests, your relationship with yourself, your intellectual life, your spiritual life, your sense of meaning or purpose, your relationship to your community. In doing this scan of your life, does any area call out for attention because it is out of balance? In each area, ask yourself if you are holding on to anything that you no longer need. What are the benefits that you get from holding on? Perhaps a sense of security or control or protection? What do you think or fear would happen if you let go of this protection? Are you ready to let go?

In conducting this exercise with hundreds of people over the years, I have seen a variety of answers to the question, "What are you holding on to?" I hear things like: friends I have outgrown, work I don't enjoy, possessions I never use, too much work, eating too much, doing too much for my kids, an inflated view of myself, my image as a rebel, my fear of displeasing my parents. People report that they hold on for a variety of reasons: "I get to be a nice guy"; "I get to feel like a martyr"; "I get people to tell me I'm wonderful"; "My kids think I'm a hero"; "We get to have a swimming pool"; "People don't expect much from me"; "I feel safe"; "I feel in control"; "I avoid conflict"; and so forth.

Just do the exercise without thinking too much or trying to be logical. Awareness of your patterns and feelings often leads to a natural rebalancing of your priorities. When you acknowledge the gap between where you are and where you want to be, this leads to acceptance, which leads to understanding, which ultimately leads to change.

Becoming aware of how you are holding on to an outdated attitude, behavior, or picture of yourself is the first stage of change. It's the "Something isn't right" stage. This sets the other seven stages into motion. Then it's important to stay aware of your feelings so you can modulate the pace of the change. Fast change is not necessarily better than slow change. If you push yourself too hard, you might scare yourself and wind up retreating. Sometimes breathing slowly and deeply as you feel where you are in the change process can help speed things along. Nudging yourself is okay, but don't force it.

Addiction to Perfection

As we well know, it is difficult for many people to let go of the need to look good, appear in control, or otherwise be perfect. Jungian analyst Marion Woodman has found through her work with high-achievers that this "addiction to perfection" masks an inner terror—"a fear of being out of control and of the chaos that will descend upon them as soon as their rigid daily routine is completed." Letting go of your addiction to perfection can be a long, but rewarding, journey.

Meta-Skill Builder 7: Valuing Your Failures

To begin this journey, start by identifying every single mistake you can remember making. Now note how each mistake was the catalyst for some lesson that you would not have received otherwise. Look for the value or utility of your failures, mistakes, and imperfections. Did you realize that most people learn more from their failures than from their successes? And the bigger the mistake, the more important the lesson.

Reframe Disasters as Learning Opportunities

When we are in our Security/Control mode, we try to maintain a sense of security by denying the things that take us out of this state. Unfortunately, as we saw earlier in this chapter, when we resist these things, we become all the more vulnerable to their influence. With the Learning/Discovery attitude, there is no need to hang on to a positive experience—because the next one can be just as rewarding. You can learn to take pleasure in every experience. Beauty really is in the eye of the beholder. And you have choice about how to use your eyes. Always remember, if you can't take pleasure in it just now, you can at least learn from it.

To reframe your perception of a painful or unwanted past experience, take a mental snapshot of the situation as you initially perceived it, and then put it in a different frame—one that views the situation from a different angle or one that includes parts of the picture that weren't visible from your first vantage point. Reframing enables you to see the situation as useful or helpful in some way. Let's say you have just missed a plane that was supposed to take you to an important meeting. That is a pretty unfortunate situation to be in, right? How might this catastrophe be reframed? Here are a few ideas:

- You can focus on how lucky you are that another plane to your destination is due to depart in only thirty minutes.
- You can use it at the meeting, relating the "funny thing that happened on the way here" to demonstrate how unflappable you are.
- You can note that you needed a little extra time before arriving at the meeting to get really prepared—and now you are forced to take that time.
- You can use it to help you develop a better plan for getting to the airport on time—so this won't happen again.

What if you aren't able to get yourself to see the situation any differently? What if your mind just won't let go of the feeling "This is awful—I'll be flustered when I get there—and people will think I'm disorganized—it's a real catastrophe!" If you have a tendency to hold on like this, then you need to diligently practice the art of reframing. But start with an incident that doesn't feel quite so serious to you—like forgetting to take out the garbage.

Meta-Skill Builder 8: Practicing Reframing

To help you practice the art of reframing, think of the large and small unwanted events or failures of your life, in both love and work. On a piece of paper, list these in a column down the left half of the page.

Now in the right column write what you learned from this experience. Rank the magnitude of the mistakes, and the magnitude of the lessons learned: put one star next to the little failures, two stars next to the medium-size failures, and three stars next to the really big, costly mistakes.

Do the same with the lessons: put one star next to the little lessons, two next to the medium-size lessons, and three stars next to the major lessons that you'll never forget. Did the three-star failures tend to provide you with three-star lessons? This idea brings to mind one of my favorite quotes from Winston Churchill: "Play for more than you can afford to lose—and you will learn the game."

2. Fear of the Past Repeating Itself

The fear that some painful or traumatic episode from our past may repeat itself creates resistance to letting go. If you were punished or criticized every time you told the unpleasant truth, you may carry into your present life a fear of telling people things that are difficult to hear. If you were rarely left alone to do things in your own way, you may resist being asked to do things by your employer or your mate.

Try treating your fear or resistance as useful information, not as something to be banished or suppressed. If you were punished in the past for asserting your needs, and you notice a tendency in the present to shy away from self-assertion, being aware of this can help you reevaluate your automatic reactions. When you look to see how similar the present situation really is to what you experienced in the past, you may discover that the two situations are significantly different and should not be lumped together in your mind. It is useful to know your typical fear reactions so that you can approach each new situation as an opportunity for this kind of reevaluation. Reevaluating such fears enables us to let them go.

Usually, upon careful examination, the present situation is quite different from the past, even though it may seem superficially similar. For example, let's take the situation where you were punished as a child for contradicting your parents. Now you are being asked to give feedback to a superior on a briefing she just presented. You are reluctant to share any comments that could be perceived as critical.

To discover if it really is appropriate to withhold your true opinion, try using this dilemma as an opportunity to learn more about your habitual reaction patterns. Look at the beliefs that underlie the fear. Do you believe that if you tell the truth you will be punished? What, specifically, do you fear when you think of being punished? Is it not being approved of, not being asked to do this type of work again, not being thought of as competent, not being trusted? What do you believe you will lose? Some people might fear losing their job, which they fear would mean losing their livelihood, which would mean losing their home, which would mean losing their family, which would lead to loss of love, self-worth, and possibly their reason for living. How far do you take your fears? It can be quite revealing to look at the specific beliefs that keep you holding on to outdated habit patterns.

Usually, when you look carefully at your fears, you discover one of two things that can help you release yourself from their power: either (1) you see how unfounded they are in reality (you will not get fired for telling your boss how to improve her presentation); or (2) you see that even if the feared thing were to happen (e.g., she won't pay attention to me or approve of me anymore), you do not need the other person in the same way you did as a child. (You are no longer dependent on the attention or approval of the authority figure the way you were when you were small.)

Valuing fears and resistances as information gives you the opportunity to reevaluate these habits, let them go, and update your perceptions of what you presently need for your safety and security.

3. Fixating on Things We Cannot Control

Many of us replay our past mistakes over and over in our minds. You did a less-than-perfect job at something. You made a social faux pas. You made a bad investment. You hurt a loved one. It is common to ruminate about such things.

When someone insults you or hurts your feelings, this, too, can occupy your mind for hours. If your thinking is focused on how best to deal with the situation, this can be useful. But once you have done all you can, it is time to turn your attention to things you can control and let go of those you cannot do anything more about. Too often, our thinking becomes obsessive, crowding the mind with so much useless stuff that there is little room left for creativity.

In a world of nonstop change, you cannot afford to have your mind going off in all directions. You need all your attention available to focus on the task of the moment.

It takes mental discipline to release the unwanted thoughts that grip our attention. Developing such discipline requires intention and work. First, you need to decide that you want to learn to let go of the worry/regret habit. It is a habit like most other habits: you learned it unconsciously and involuntarily, which makes it very hard to control consciously and voluntarily. Thus, you will need to find something else to do with your mind instead of ruminating—something else to focus your attention on in order to free your mind of unnecessary chatter.

To keep your attention available for dealing with present reality, focus on what you do have control over, so you can let go of what you do not. This is not as easy as it sounds. Let's consider it in more depth.

My need to control the events and people around me lessens when I feel in control of myself. When I can't maintain control, then my need to control *others* seems to increase. The other night, for example, I was rewriting a particularly difficult section of this book. Every time I would feel frustrated or stuck in my creative process, I would hit the SAVE button on my keyboard, get up and go down to the kitchen, open the refrigerator door, get out some food, eat it hungrily but without really tasting it, wash my dishes, and come back up to my computer—all without seeing, feeling, or thinking about what I was doing. At the end of the evening, I felt stuffed, having no idea how many times I had repeated this sequence. All I know is that I was definitely out of control of my inner state.

So how do you think I approached my outer world the next day as I facilitated a group of managers who were struggling with how to communicate with their employees about a proposed restructuring? Instead of practicing what I preach by allowing them to discover their own answers to their dilemma, I started giving advice. I noticed that they kept cutting me off and trying to wrest control away from me, but I found it very difficult to let go. You see, I had a bad time with compulsive overeating the night before, so my game was off the following day.

My frustration with my inner chaos or lack of control got projected outward onto my environment. Needless to say, I had a lot of amends to make after that in order to regain the trust of that group of managers.

4 . Addictions and Compulsions

I have proposed that the less in control you are of your inner world the more you feel the need to control your outer world. To see if this is true for you, take another look at your list of what you do control, and notice what happens when you let yourself down in one of these areas.

Does your need to control others increase in proportion?

When you aren't getting enough sleep or exercise, are you more demanding and less flexible with your coworkers? Or perhaps more self-critical or perfectionistic?

When you have overworked, overeaten, or overindulged, are you more impatient with your mate or your kids? Do you find it more difficult to shift plans?

Alcoholics and people with compulsive personality disorders tend to be more controlling of others than people who are not so addicted. This is because compulsive behavior (lack of inner control) makes one vulnerable to the high need to control the external world.

When I talk about alcoholic and other compulsive behavior, I am not singling out a small segment of the population. We live in an addiction-prone society. I believe that those with serious problems are simply bellwethers of the direction in which our society as a whole is headed.

Most people I know exhibit some degree of compulsive behavior and a fair degree of defensiveness or denial about it. Such behavior is an unconscious attempt to manage their anxiety about feeling out of control, to gain a sense of control in at least some small segment of their lives. It is as if a person is saying, "If I can't feel in charge, at least I can get high or relax, or feel good for a short time, and I can do so predictably and,reliably. It has the same effect every time." The ways people get high are myriad. Often the high is not even pleasurable, but at least it provides a temporary escape from anxiety, a temporary sense of being in control.

What is your "high" or your way of getting a fairly predictable, although fleeting and illusory, sense of control? In addition to the familiar answers such as food, alcohol, drugs, sex, gambling, sleeping, tobacco, and emotional outbursts, we could also add such socially sanctioned compensations as work, shopping, television, music, driving, movies, and video and computer games. The list keeps growing. Anything you can do, you can do too much.

The need to control others and one's external world (including the need to get high) creates a vicious and ever-worsening cycle: your need for control makes you prone to frustration because there is less and less in your external world that you can control. This frustration leads to impulsive/compulsive behavior, such as the escapes listed in the preceding paragraph. Impulsive/compulsive behavior leads to feeling even less in control of yourself, which leads you to feel an even greater need to control your external world, which we know is an increasingly frustrating proposition. This sequence repeats itself over and over.

In Chapter Four, I introduced the idea that it is possible to feel oneself as part of the larger flow of life, and that this brings with it a sense of trust in the face of chaos. Researcher Mihaly Csikszentmihalyi, in his best-seller entitled *Flow,* defines flow as "that optimal state of consciousness wherein one achieves happiness through control over one's inner life." He surveyed thousands of people, asking them to describe what they were doing when they felt a sense of mastery or of being in control in their lives. What Csikszentmihalyi found, after studying thousands of people from all walks of life and from a variety of cultures, was that a person feels in control to the extent that she has developed the ability to control her own consciousness moment by moment.

It appears that what people are really seeking when they attempt to control others or get a predictable, controllable high, is an inner sense of well-being or happiness. Failing this, they resort to controlling the people and things around them.

How we feel about ourselves and the happiness we get from our work and relationships depends ultimately on our attitudes and on our ability to take charge of our inner experience. How we make ourselves is much more important in this regard than how we make a living.

We can resist or embrace anything that happens to us. Our awareness of this choice, and our ability to exercise it, makes all the difference.

How can you gain control of your inner state so you can let go of compulsively controlling external events and people? First, you need to make this a priority in your life. Then, you need to select a vehicle that fits your lifestyle and personality. Here are some of the more well known vehicles to inner mastery:

1. *Twelve-step programs.* Alcoholics (and others plagued by compulsive self-defeating habits) typically have an underdeveloped capacity for controlling some of their impulses. As these people develop more inner self-mastery through a twelve-step program, one of the frequent benefits is that their need to control others decreases. For information on these programs, consult your local telephone directory.

2. *Mental disciplines like meditation.* Over fifteen hundred years ago, Indian yogis developed meditation and yogic disciplines to calm, balance, and attune the inner self. Many of these practices are now being taught in the West. For an overview of these various practices, consult S. Z. Klausner's *The Quest for Self-Control.* (This book and others mentioned here are referenced in the bibliography at the end of the book. For an introductory self-help program on how to begin a meditation practice, see David Harp's *New Three Minute Meditator.*)

3. *Body-oriented disciplines like martial arts and sports.* (See Michael Murphy's *The Future of the Body* and Deane Juhan's *Job's Body.*)

4. *Daily life as spiritual practice.* A craft (art, music, writing, dance) can be a form of inner work. So can your vocation or avocation. (See Carla Needleman's *Work of Craft.*)

5. *Biofeedback processes.* Brain waves or other psychophysiological processes can be recorded and transmitted back to you as a way of teaching you to monitor your internal state. (See Davis, Eshelman, and McKay's *Relaxation and Stress Reduction Workbook.*)

Anything you can do, you can learn to do more consciously. To the extent that you are present to yourself in your moment-to-moment awareness, you tend to feel more in control no matter what your outer circumstances. You also tend to be more effective in manifesting your goals and intentions.

There is a paradox here: as you master your own inner chaos, you become more accepting of the chaos in your surroundings. Thus, if you wish to let go of your need to control others, exert more self-discipline.

5. Suppressing Feelings

I do a lot of work with police officers. One of the more interesting aspects of my job is the opportunity to accompany the officers as a "ride-along." I ride in the squad car as they go about responding to the various crises and everyday problems that occur during their work shift. From talking with them about the more dangerous aspects of their work, I have observed a fascinating phenomenon. When a cop has experienced something traumatic on the job, like getting shot at or heckled, he is less likely to develop a post-traumatic stress reaction if he has the opportunity to talk about the situation right away.

I know from my work as a psychotherapist and company doctor that this principle holds true also for ordinary "civilians" in their jobs and relationships. People can get beyond their traumatic reactions faster if they have a chance to vent them. Venting feelings with someone who has been through the experience with you, like other cops on the SWAT team, can be especially helpful.

There is a fundamental principle of change operating here: what you can feel, you can heal. Expressing feelings is a form of letting go. You are letting out a part of yourself that you might be reluctant to reveal for fear of looking weak or vulnerable. By letting it out, you are accepting what happened to you and affirming that your feelings about the situation are valid.

Accepting a situation, even a pretty awful one, enables you to deal with it internally so you can get on with whatever is next. Not accepting it keeps you holding on to either the belief that you can't handle thinking about it, or to the wish that it never happened— which of course prevents you from coming to terms with it. If you can't accept something as it is, you will feel out of control in relation to it. Simple acceptance gives us some measure of control.

Some people find it most helpful to express their feelings to other people. Others write their feelings in a journal. Some even use a tape recorder. You may wish to try all three ways to see which works best for you.

Meta-Skill Builder 9:
Exercising Your "Feeling Muscles"

To help you develop your ability to feel difficult-to-feel feelings, complete the following sentence stems with as many different answers as you can think of for each stem. To help you get started, I have included a few responses that others have given in parentheses next to each item.

I like _____ (attention, being left alone, freedom, my life).

I love _____ (making love, sunsets over the ocean, beauty).

I don't like _____ (self-centered people, my weight, time pressure).

I want _____ (to be liked, a lot of money, to help people).

I don't want _____ (to grow old, to lose my job, any more kids).

I feel good about _____ (my looks, how I'm treated at work).

I feel passionate about _____ (telling the truth, saving the earth).

I feel bad about _____ (all the money I have lost, my divorce, my failing memory).

I detest _____ (my mother-in-law, arrogant people, laziness).

I feel good when _____ (I'm dancing, I'm driving, my baby is sleeping contentedly).

I feel bad when _____ (I'm late for appointments, I let someone down, I overeat).

I need _____ (love, something to believe in, to be more disciplined.)

I don't need _____ (any more work, people telling me what to do).

I'm sick and tired of _____ (my mate's complaints, not being appreciated).

I long for _____ (work that I feel inspired by, someone I can really love, time to think my own thoughts).

I wish _____ (I were smarter, I hadn't gone into this field, I knew then what I know now).

When you do this exercise, it is as if you are working a set of muscles that you may not be used to using. Your "feeling muscles" will get stronger from use. Do not try to interpret your answers or draw conclusions about yourself. See if you can just let yourself write what you feel without any goal in mind. If you are a person who tends to suppress feelings, do this exercise often. It will help you learn to let go more easily, and it will give your personality more definition and clarity. Expressing feelings helps you accept who you are and feel okay about it.

6. Attempting to Control Others

Many of your biggest challenges in practicing the art of letting go will be in your dealings with coworkers, bosses, and customers. You want and expect them to behave one way, and they do the opposite.

Have you ever been in a disagreement where the more forcefully you put forth your views, the more the other person did the same? But when you showed more interest in the other's viewpoint, then this person listened to yours? Or perhaps you have noticed with some people that the more you try to get them to do things your way, the more they resist; but when you trust them to do things in their way, the more open they are to you. These situations demonstrate how the intent to control others creates resistance, whereas the intent to learn about others creates openness.

If you are willing to take responsibility for the fact that how someone treats you depends in part upon whether this person feels respected by you, then you are in position to foster openness in your relationships with others.

Let's say one of your teammates is unable to accept work-related feedback without overreacting. This person, Paul, has such thin skin that every time you get near him, you seem to brush up against one of his sensitive spots. Have you ever known anyone like this? Here is how letting go of control can transform this situation from negative to positive. First, you need to let go of your need for Paul to be any different than he is. If you accept him and the situation just as it is without resentment or blame, he will feel your respect for him, which will help him be more open to you. Then you need to let go again, this time letting go of the way you have always related to Paul. Envision relating to him in the way his sensitive reactions are telling you *he prefers to be treated,* even if this feels awkward or foreign to you.

Letting go in this instance means letting go of your attachment to doing things in *your usual style.* If you learn from Paul that he is especially sensitive to a particular tone of voice, for example, you may choose to refrain from using this tone around him. By doing this, you are treating him respectfully in *his* terms, not *yours.* You are letting go of your usual way of doing things in order to develop a good working relationship. It is your decision to do this, not his, so you are still in charge of your own choices.

In the new workplace, you need to be able to work with all types of people. This involves letting go of any attachment you might have to a particular style of doing things so that you can learn from each individual how he or she prefers to be dealt with, delegated to, or supervised. Chapter Seven will consider in depth how to develop working relationships built on respect for each individual's uniqueness.

How Letting Go Can Make You Indispensable to Your Organization and Customers

How can your ability to let go add significantly and noticeably to your value in the new workplace? As we have seen, attachment to wishes and oughts clouds our ability to perceive current reality; whereas the ability to see and acknowledge our actual situation allows us to do whatever it takes to deal with the situation or solve the problem.

1. "Whatever it takes" often includes seeking help from other people, other departments, other companies. The ability to seek and receive help gracefully can add immeasurably to your power in the organization. You have access to more knowledge, and you build stronger relationships in the process. When you seek an-

other's help, you are in effect saying, "I value you enough to want to learn from you." This builds a cooperative alliance that you can draw on in the future. In today's complex workplace, you need all the linkages you can create. You never know when you might have occasion to interact with this other person in an entirely different context—perhaps even a potentially unfriendly situation. If you already have a positive relationship with this person, you have something in reserve to draw on.

2. If you are a manager or supervisor, review the control processes that are in place, either in a customer relations function or in a group of people who report to you. Look for ways of turning more control over to the customer, or the employees, thereby empowering them to solve problems as these occur. This releases you to pay attention to other issues. You gain control of more of your time. They gain a sense of power and self-responsibility. Your organization gains because more people are feeling responsible and taking leadership.

Meta-Skill Builder 10: Interviewing "Letting Go" Role Models

3. Make a list of people in authority positions (in your organization or in those you interface with) who seem to have mastered the art of letting go. Write up some questions you would like to ask these people. Then call at least five of them and ask for an interview. Doing this accomplishes three things: you learn what others have done to help them let go; in seeking ideas from others, you are practicing letting go and receiving help; and you establish positive relationships with key people in your work environment.

How Letting Go Can Help You Prevent or Respond to Crisis

1. The ability to let go of what is no longer working so that something more appropriate can take its place is critical in a society undergoing rapid, often traumatic, change—because it helps you manage the anxiety that invariably accompanies the break-

down of familiar forms. People who cannot let go will be so overcome by anxiety that they will regress into comfortable but dysfunctional addictions and ways of thinking. They will apply old solutions to new problems. They will attempt to control situations that are beyond their control rather than responding and creatively adapting.

2. Letting go of the need to be single-handedly in control is going to be even more important as the diversity within our world increases. If we do not respect the interests of "have not" or disenfranchised groups, those who feel they have nothing to lose could "bring the house down" on the rest of us. You need to be able to see your proposed solution from a number of vantage points. In order to do this, you will need to be able to ask for help and input from a variety of sources so you can predict how your idea is likely to affect and be perceived by people whose realities are different from yours. You will only be prepared to honor and include these inputs if you have let go of your need to have things go "your way."

And Remember...

- The key to learning is allowing yourself to feel insecure and "out of control."
- When you include *feeling uncomfortable* within your definition of *being in control,* you greatly expand your ability to cope with change and crisis.
- When you pay attention to and master the things in your life that you can control, your mind lets go of trying to control the uncontrollable.
- You can frame, or reframe, anything that happens in a variety of ways. You can see the same situation as a comedy or a tragedy, a catastrophe or a learning experience.
- You can resist or embrace anything that happens to you, such as other peoples' frustrating behavior. Your awareness of that choice, and your ability to exercise it, spells the difference between empowerment and powerlessness.

Focus on Essentials

In a world of continual endings and new beginnings, we need some constant point to focus on, a center around which to gather our learnings. Our connection with our essence provides such a stable point of reference. When your essence finds expression in your work, everything you do has more clarity, power, and vitality.

If you want to be truly open to learning, you need to know who you are, separate from your roles, responsibilities, possessions, and relationships. Knowing yourself at this essential level gives you the courage to confront the need for profound change.

I recently had the opportunity to meet and interview Tom Melohn, former CEO of North American Tool & Die and author of *The New Partnership: Bringing Out the Best in Your People, Customers, Profits, and Yourself.*

Melohn's is the story of a man who had it all—wealthy parents, prep school and Ivy League education, early success, self-confidence, brains, guts. But at midlife, he realized that something wasn't right in his professional life, so he began to search within himself for the missing piece of the puzzle.

At the time, he was senior vice president for a *Fortune* 500 company, a position he had hoped would give him the visibility to become president of one of the *Fortune* 500. But he felt frustrated, alone, and out of place. He felt he was living a lie.

"Since childhood, I had dreamed of becoming CEO of one of the *Fortune* 500. When other kids were memorizing baseball statistics, I was researching the names and success qualifications of CEO's. . . .

It was not easy to just let go of that dream. I was so close. I knew I could get there if I could just keep doing what I was doing.

"I finally had to admit that my life was a lie. I was always at odds with the top people at 'corporate.' They expected me to come out with five new products in eighteen months, and they didn't care what I had to do or who I had to step on to get it done. The time frames were unrealistic—if it was going to be done right. No one cared how you got it done as long as you got it done on time. I was expected to put a little 'spin' on things to make them come out looking right. I couldn't be honest under those rules. This was eating me up inside. The first value I knew I had to live by was honesty."

At age forty-five, on the verge of attaining his childhood dream, he was fired because he was "too disruptive." Melohn decided he had to make a change. He could no longer pretend that this was the life he wanted—in spite of its many perks. He thought, "Where can I go where I can live my life consistent with who I am? So I said, 'To hell with the corporate image of success, I'm going to live my values.'" And so he made the decision to abandon his lifelong dream of becoming CEO of a *Fortune* 500 company.

Shortly after Melohn made that life-changing decision to live in accord with his inner values, an unexpected opportunity came his way. He and a colleague had a chance to purchase a struggling company in San Leandro, California—North American Tool & Die. They bought it, and Melohn became its CEO.

At that time, NATD was like many smaller manufacturers—marginally profitable, its workforce unenthusiastic. Nor did the future look especially bright, since a number of longtime employees were exploring greener pastures.

Today the situation is much different. Company sales are triple and profits six times what they were in 1978, when Melohn took over. "The average pretax profit for other companies in our industry is three and a half percent. Ours is twenty percent," Melohn reports proudly.

He believes that success is a by-product of knowing who you are and behaving accordingly. If you live in harmony with who you are, you will be happy and fulfilled. In our conversation, he talked about such essential values as honesty, trust, mutual respect, dignity, and caring.

"At North American, we were up front about how much everyone was paid, for example. You never ask about pay in any preemployment interview, right? I would bring it up in the first interview. I would give the applicant a pay schedule of every employee. Everybody knows everyone else's pay anyway. I wanted to get it up front to eliminate the suspicion that someone is making more than someone else on a particular job. Plus, what was I doing? I was saying what you see is what you get, man. Honesty. You talk about values. It's the little things, the little things."

As he continued to tell the story of how he rediscovered the essential values that were to guide the rest of his life, he talked about trust—the trust that builds when you do what you say you are going to do for people. "We promised the employees that the company would pay all the medical and dental and life insurance, and we did. The insurance people said, 'You're out of your minds.' But we made a deal. We made a deal, didn't we?" He told how he trusted employees with "unlocked" telephones, which led them to want to honor this trust.

Then he spoke of mutual respect: "Why do we need the big office? Why do we need separate dining? To prove that we are better than somebody else? Did you read in *Barbarians at the Gate* about RJR? Remember the private airport at Winston-Salem with incredibly expensive original artwork and oriental rugs? Who are we trying to impress? The employees have what—linoleum, cafeteria, cubicles? They're treated like a number. That's not mutual respect."

And finally, he spoke about caring: "When we see one of our fellow employees heading south, we try to help. Sit down with them, 'Hey, what's the matter, weren't the instructions right? Machine not working?' Without crossing the line, 'Is there anything we can help you with at home? We want to help. You're hurting, it's hurting all of us. We want to work with you.'"

Melohn's first forty years were spent pursuing the proverbial brass ring. He then spent the next twenty years searching for ways to bring his actions in line with his inner, or essential, self.

At the end of the search, he found what had been there all along—some basic, simple values that gave coherence and meaning to his life because they were connected with his essence. Listening to him tell his personal version of the hero's journey, I said to myself, "Here is a truly happy man."

Melohn's story illustrates the profound changes that can occur as we live more in harmony with our essential values and purpose. This chapter will focus on how to discover the *essential self* that is seeking expression through you and how to bring more of that self to your work.

Discovering our essence requires honesty—honesty about who we are, what we think and feel, and what we stand for. We cannot *learn about* ourselves if we are not willing to *be* ourselves.

Lest we judge ourselves too harshly, let us remember that it is not so easy to both be in a relationship (including a relationship to a company) and stay entirely true to ourselves. The more dependent we are on this other entity (person, group, or organization), the harder it is to differentiate ourselves from it and behave authentically.

An honest relationship involves a continual dialogue process about how to meet the needs of all concerned. All parties continually learn and grow through confronting differences. If we need the relationship for our "survival," honesty is sacrificed to our fears. To avoid rocking the boat, we deny the things we would rather not deal with.

We saw examples of denial in previous chapters in the "Everything's all right" or "everything's gonna be all right" palliatives. When we are too dependent on the other for our sense of well-being, we may tell ourselves that everything we are being asked to do is okay—even if it violates our inner sense of rightness. Denial is not something we do consciously. It is the way we avoid any pain we fear might be too much for us—in this case the pain of feeling it is not safe to authentically express ourselves.

Denial is a lie we tell ourselves to make our present situation tolerable or to justify our position on some issue—because we do not trust ourselves to deal with something new, unknown, or different. Denial can get to be a habit when it becomes easier for us to lie to ourselves than to stand up to others.

When we stay connected to that source of inner truth called the essential self, it becomes easier to break the denial habit.

This chapter is based upon four central ideas:

1. The human personality has a superficial layer, *the conditioned self,* and a deeper layer, *the essential self.* Your essential self is not the product of conditioning. It is the part of your being that would remain if you could shed habitual, protective patterns acquired in childhood. In order to learn from any interaction, your essential self must be present. Otherwise, you will simply add to the superficial layer of your personality—the layer that identifies with your unexamined habits and reactions and behaves as if that's all there is.

2. Humans have a basic need to express their essential values and talents in their work. Your work is your way of participating in creating a better world. It is your vehicle for finding your uniquely right place in the human family. It is an antidote to alienation and loneliness.

3. It is possible to express your essential self in your work, even if your job duties do not explicitly call for these essential qualities. When you do this, you gain an inner stability that is not easily threatened by changes in your work environment. Then everything you do has more clarity, power, and juice.

4. Curiosity is the hallmark of the essential self. At your core, you are essentially a learning organism. Everything you do at work, including your mistakes, provides grist for the mill of learning about yourself—about who you are, what your gifts are, and how to more effectively offer these gifts.

Most companies do not encourage much honest self-expression in their workforces—even if they have a company vision statement that says they do. But in the new workplace, our jobs can and must include more of the whole person. Otherwise, learning cannot occur—for ourselves or the organization. In order to create relationships where learning can take place, we must bring our essential selves to the interaction.

The Essential Self

Your essential self is at the core of your being. It is often referred to as the true or real self, as distinguished from the self you usually present to the world. It is the self you were born to become. It is who you would be if your character were undistorted by cultural conditioning and unadulterated by parental injunctions. It shines through in your values, your sense of purpose, and your drive to express yourself authentically through your work.

Your essential self is the "seed" that contains your potential. Just as the acorn contains the genetic information for becoming an oak tree, humans possess not only physical, but also emotional, mental, and spiritual predispositions. Some of these potentials are obvious. Others you continue to discover over the course of a lifetime. At any given point in time, you are in the process of discovering, expressing, and expanding these potentials.

The essential self is open—like a natural, healthy child. But it also has a shape to it that is uniquely you. It is not who your parents wanted you to be or who they feared you might become. That would be your *conditioned self.* Your essence is based on something deeper and more unchanging than most of what you may have learned about yourself from others in childhood.

Becoming aware of an unfolding purpose for your life empowers you to make choices that further that purpose. You are less easily blown off course by the winds of information overload, other's unreasonable expectations, or your own insecurities. Knowing and acting in accord with your essential self gives everything you do an added measure of stability, credibility, and authority. By the way, the word "authority" is derived from the Greek, *authentikós,* "by one's own hand." To be author of one's own life, to write one's own script, is the work of reclaiming the essential self. When you are connected with your essential self, you communicate a powerful sense of inner authority.

There are several steps on the way to bringing more of your essential self to work:

1. Learn to recognize the difference between your essential self and your conditioned self, and to stay connected to your essence.
2. Identify the essential values that support your essential self.
3. Discover ways to express your essence at work through your "essential vocation."

1. Recognize the Difference Between the Essential Self and the Conditioned Self

If you can imagine what you might have been like as a child if your environment had totally supported you in seeing, feeling, and doing things in your own unique way, that will give you a clue to your essence.

A basic quality of the essential self is openness to learning and discovery. Have you noticed how very young children, when they encounter something unfamiliar, will be drawn to touch, examine, smell, taste, and even to eat the object of their curiosity? The essential self is a lot like this child. She is driven to explore and really engage with the world around her.

Like the child, the essential self tends to express itself according to its own inner blueprint, which may not always conform to the way most people do things. While it does not look to others for its sense of well-being, it is in no way antisocial. It has a strong sense of connection to others, but it expresses this connection in its own unique way.

When we are identified with the conditioned self, our attitudes and behavior mimic the Security/Control posture. When we depend on others for our sense of well-being, as we do in Security/Control, we have a strong need to appear in control, to look good, and to refrain from rocking the boat. The conditioned self is tense most of the time because it rests on the shaky foundation of other people's opinions.

The big problem with the way our personalities are structured is this: We believe that our conditioned self is who we really are. We put so much energy into protecting ourselves from the fears of the conditioned self that we feel disconnected and alienated from our essence and therefore from others. We don't trust ourselves, and we don't trust each other.

During our formative years, we received many messages that told us who we were and who we should be. Many of these messages were sent unconsciously by adults to keep us from making them uncomfortable. The result was a self that was limited in its full expression by a number of learned habit patterns or self-limiting beliefs. Often these beliefs caused us to doubt our lovability, our worth, or our capability. We then went through the rest of our lives acting as if these self-doubts were really true of us—and trying to hide these doubts from others.

To discover how your concept of yourself was conditioned by your early environment, start way back when you were a child growing up in your parent's home. What was life like for you then? Get an image of what you were like and how you were treated. Were you seen as the responsible child in your family, the one whom your parents could depend on to be good, to do what you were asked to do, to help out around the house? Or perhaps you were the clown, the rebel, the invisible one, or even the problem child or scapegoat.

Often we learn to play certain roles in our families, roles that carry over into our adult lives. Your role or script reveals an underlying belief about how the world works and how the world and other people are predisposed toward you. This script is part of your conditioned self. This is the layer that most people identify with, believing it is who they really are.

Each family is like a miniature culture. In most families every member is expected to behave according to certain unwritten rules, rules such as "Don't show weakness"; "Don't attract attention to yourself"; "Don't do anything foolish"; "Don't ever owe anything to anyone"; "Don't let anyone take advantage of you." Such admonitions become part of the conditioned self. When such rules are carried over into adulthood, they limit our options and skew our perceptions. Later on, we join companies that have unwritten rules similar to those in our families.

Often, when your early learning has reinforced a particular pattern of thought or behavior, you tend to encounter problems in later life that call attention to the fact that you have overidentified with this pattern, that you have taken it on as your true identity when it is simply your conditioning.

Paula was the oldest of four siblings in a family headed by a workaholic father and an alcoholic mother. In this environment, she became the "responsible one." Throughout her life, she played out this unconscious script, often saying yes when she really felt like saying no. Others saw her as generous and caring, "not a selfish bone in her body." She automatically identified with this characterization. At midlife, as head of a community service agency, she realized she was carrying the bulk of the load for the entire agency staff. It was her grant that paid their salaries, and they were doing very little to support and maintain this funding. Her caseload was double anyone else's. When she saw the predicament she was in, she recognized it as a script she had adopted in childhood as a means of survival. She knew she needed to unlearn her habit of indiscriminately taking care of other people, so she could care for and express herself.

Recurring negative experiences like Paula's can be useful because they reveal to us where our learning has been lopsided or unbalanced. If your conditioning taught you to appear always strong and independent, for example, you may get upset with weakness and dependency in others. You may find yourself frequently at odds with this more dependent type of person, for reasons you can't explain. This can happen in both love and work relationships. The problem you are having reveals where your development has been lopsided, what you need to learn in order to feel more whole or more connected with your essence. Sometimes what you need to learn involves developing or manifesting some latent talent or resource. Other times it means letting go of fears or *self-limiting beliefs*.

Paula, in the example above, carried a self-limiting belief that her worthiness was based on taking care of other people, and a *fear* that if she said no, she was being a bad person, and would be punished. To reconnect with her essential self, she would have to question her beliefs and fears, see where they originated, and reevaluate their validity in light of her present situation. In doing this, she might realize, for example, that her staff members are not dependent on her the way her brothers and sister were, and that doing too much for her staff is disempowering.

Meta-Skill Builder 11: The X-Ray Process

Here is an exercise to help you discover your own lopsidedness and release the self-limiting beliefs of the conditioned self. I call it the X-Ray Process because it enables you to look under the surface layers of your personality to see the beliefs, fears, and unconscious assumptions that drive much of your behavior. Once people become conscious of these underlying beliefs and fears, and replace them with more appropriate thoughts, they become free to express the essential self.

1. A recurring unwanted or unexplainable event or theme in my life is _____. Here are some examples:

- people don't listen to me
- people don't treat me with respect
- people are intimidated by me
- people resent me
- people expect me to take care of them
- people leave me, abandon me, betray me
- people always want more than I can give
- people don't trust me to do things on my own
- people try to control me or limit my autonomy
- people don't expect enough of me
- people criticize me
- I can't get enough attention, acknowledgement, respect, etc.
- I rarely finish what I start
- I don't takes risks because I am afraid of being hurt or making mistakes
- I jump into things too soon and later have regrets

2. How I participate in creating this negative outcome is _____. Examples:

- I don't listen to myself
- I don't treat myself with respect
- I am afraid of others
- I resent others
- I betray myself; I don't stand up for and support myself
- I expect too much of myself

3. As a child, I was seen as or treated as _____. Examples:

- a pest
- a perfect child

- a troublemaker
- the problem child
- the irresponsible one
- the clown
- frail and sickly
- strong
- the smart one
- the pretty one

4. Because of how I was seen as a child I tend to be too _____ and not _____ enough.
Examples:

- conformist . . . original
- weak . . . strong
- strong . . . weak
- competent . . . helpless
- efficient . . . playful

5. I am especially sensitive to being treated as if _____.
Examples:

- I don't know what I'm doing
- I'm inferior
- I am the strong one, the one who can handle any problem
- I am not to be taken seriously
- I have all the answers
- I don't have feelings
- I have it easier than others
- it's my fault when things go wrong
- my voice doesn't count

6. This may be because I harbor a fear or self-limiting belief that _____.
Examples:

- I don't know what I'm doing
- I'm inferior
- I'm unlovable or unworthy

- no one can handle the problem as well as I can
- I am not to be taken seriously
- I should have all the answers
- I have it easier than others
- it's my fault when things go wrong
- my voice doesn't count

7. This fear translates into a belief about people that
_____.
Examples:

- people don't trust me
- people don't like me
- people don't care about my problems
- people will use you if you let them
- people don't want to hear the truth
- people are motivated by self-interest
- people like to get their own way and will sometimes do anything to get it
- people don't care what I have to say

8. If I were open to discovering that _____, I would probably be happier and more successful.
Examples:

- people are looking for opportunities to give to me
- people will support me if I let them
- people do trust me
- people do want to hear the truth
- people want to hear what I have to say

9. To discover whether or not my self-limiting beliefs (from item 6) are (still) true, I would have to take the following risk: I would have to _____.

- speak my opinion, even if it disagrees with the majority view
- let someone do something for me
- ask someone for help

- speak up even when I'm not asked for my opinion
- wait and see if other people call me, if I don't call them

10. To help myself gain the courage to take such risks, I need
_____.

Examples:

- to feel I can learn from whatever happens
- to feel my self-esteem will not be affected by the outcome
- to remember all the other risks I have successfully survived
- to know I will be okay no matter what happens

The X-Ray Process is an exercise for identifying your self-limiting beliefs, understanding where they came from, and transforming them into positive self-affirmations.

If you take a mythologist's view of your life, you will view the difficulties and obstacles you encounter on your path as tests that the gods put in front of you to make you a stronger, better person. The goal of the mythological "hero's journey" is to uncover the unconscious conditioned responses that motivate you and to consciously choose your own responses—responses that express your essential self.

According to mythologist Joseph Campbell, "The hero is one who, while still alive, discovers the essential self which in most people remains more or less unconscious." Not everyone will choose to undertake the hero's journey. As you may have seen in doing the X-Ray Process, honestly admitting the lies you have told yourself can be quite unsettling.

The X-Ray Process also offers a perspective on how you got off course and how to get back on. It illuminates the obstacles (unwanted events) that the gods have put in your path. Your hero's journey is your discovery of how these obstacles can be grappled with, overcome, and learned from. Viewing your problems and hang-ups as heroic obstacles can give your outer life a connection to your inner, deeper purpose.

The X-Ray Process can help you release the core fear that controls you. The less controlled you are by fear, the freer you are to choose your responses to situations from a full range of options. And, as we have seen, the more free you feel, the less need you will have to control others, and the more honest you will be with both yourself and others.

When you are connected to your essence, you feel connected to others even when they do things that don't please you. If you get an unfavorable performance review, for example (or if it is your task to deliver one), you use the situation to further your connection with the other and with yourself by asking, "What can I learn about myself from this situation, or this other person, to help me be more fully who I am?"

Recall some negative feedback you have received from a supervisor, coworker, or customer. Now see if you can focus on the information this feedback contained about yourself and about the person giving the feedback. How can you use this information to more effectively serve this person in the future?

When you focus on your essence instead of your ego, you do not take negative feedback as a personal attack. You see it as useful for your learning—both about yourself and about the person delivering the message.

Growing into maturity involves giving up our dependency on others to tell us what is right for us. When we take back the power from authorities outside ourselves to define who we are and how we shall live, that is when we feel truly empowered. The challenges of the new workplace require great courage and self-mastery. Those who meet these challenges will be leaders in the twenty-first century.

Tips to Hasten Your Journey

Here are some things you can do to identify and get to know your essential self.

Meta-Skill Builder 12: Journaling

Keep a journal. Writing out your thoughts and feelings can be very revealing. You may notice a theme emerging as you write. You may see that there is a characteristic tone or mood to your expressions. As you "talk" to yourself in writing, you may discover that you can be your own sounding board.

Meta-Skill Builder 13: Time Out

Take time out to reflect, contemplate, or meditate. Sitting quietly, allowing your thoughts to flow without attaching significance to any of them, helps you get perspective on the events of your life.

Meta-Skill Builder 14: Conscious Breathing

Set aside time for conscious deep breathing. Breathing into the belly can help you connect to a feeling state often associated with the open innocence of childhood. Even a minute or two of this breathing can help you feel more connected to your deeper self.

Meta-Skill Builder 15: Connect with Your Infant Self

Find an old baby picture of yourself. Look into this little one's eyes to see what sense you get of its essential feeling state. If you feel moved to do so, you might also tell this little person that you intend to listen to it more often and take better care of it.

Meta-Skill Builder 16: Interview Your Inner Child

Get to know your inner child, and learn to respond to its needs. To help yourself do this, recall what it felt like to be one or two years of age. Use your intuition here, since you may not have any clear memories. Create a mental picture of yourself at this age in or near your childhood home. Conduct an imaginary interview with this little person to find out how it feels and what it needs from you.

Then envision yourself as the loving, appreciative parent that this child needs. In your mind's eye, see yourself giving to the child whatever it needs: tenderness, understanding, guidance, advice, appreciation. It can help to hold a pillow or a stuffed toy in your arms to symbolize this relationship. As the child, see and feel yourself receiving all that is being offered. Breathe deeply and take it in.

You can also write out a dialogue between inner parent and child in your journal. Allow your child part to feel and express its needs and frustrations. Let the adult part hear and validate the child's needs. (For more on this topic see Margaret Paul's *Inner Bonding: Becoming A Loving Adult to Your Inner Child.*)

Meta-Skill Builder 17:
Pay Attention to Your Dreams

Dreams reveal themes and feeling states in your unconscious mind that are calling to your conscious mind to pay attention. They often tell you about something you have been ignoring or denying.

2. Identify Your Essential Values

The first step in learning to center your life around your essential values is to discover what you value and why. Tom Melohn became aware of his essential values after experiencing deep frustration with the values he was living as he climbed the corporate ladder. He learned what *did* fit for him through the normal trial-and-error process—by discovering what *did not.*

Inventorying your values in advance of a crisis allows you to do some trial and error in your mind. You do not have to live through every situation to learn from it. Knowing your values ahead of time prepares you to quickly evaluate your options when something changes in your work environment. When you are aware of your purpose and values, it becomes easier to communicate your wishes and needs to those in decision-making positions. You are also able to spot the opportunity embedded in the crisis. In times of rapid change, new opportunities occur at a more rapid rate. If you know yourself and what you want, you are in a better position to seize these openings.

Meta-Skill Builder 18:
Values Served by Working

Ask yourself the question "Why Do I Work?" Then look at this list of values that illustrate some of the benefits people derive from working. Place one star next to all values that describe why you work. Then add one more star to those you feel more strongly about and two more stars to those you feel most strongly about.

Values List

acceptance

adventure

appreciation

autonomy

belonging

being a team player

contribution to world peace or
   justice

comfort

creativity

democratic participation

doing a good job

ecological balance in nature

fairness

fun

friendship

harmony and cooperation

health

helping others develop
   themselves

honesty

independence

integrity

intimacy

joy

justice

love of the activity itself

making a contribution

money

nurturance

open communication

order

opportunity for advancement

personal growth

perfection

power

recognition

respect

safety

security

self-esteem

sharing love and warm feelings

status

spiritual meaning

service

personal success

success of your employer

support

trust

well-being of loved ones

well-being of humanity

other values:

Make a separate list of all those values you starred more than once. Keep this list with you, and at times, during the day, reflect on the values you are aiming to serve through your work. This will help you find opportunities for expressing your values in your daily activities.

Meta-Skill Builder 19: Finding Fulfillment

Now ask yourself, What brings me fulfillment?

To look more deeply at the question of fulfillment, reflect on the following questions, and then write your answers.

Recall three or four of the best, most rewarding or fulfilling experiences of your life. Describe these experiences in detail.

What were the key ingredients that made these experiences so rewarding?

What work-related feelings are most important to you: feeling useful, feeling powerful, feeling smart, feeling as if you have achieved something significant, feeling the sense of a job well done, the feeling of having something finished, feeling in control, feeling recognized or valued, feeling challenged?

What parts of yourself do you value most highly: your physical part, your emotional part, your intellectual part, your spiritual part, your social part, your ethics, your humor, your self-discipline? What positive qualities or attributes would a best friend describe about you?

Which parts do you value least? What aspects of your self do you give least time and attention to? What are you critical of?

How do you express your most valued qualities in your activities, both at home and at work? Reflect back on your activities of the past week or two, noting when and how you have utilized the parts and qualities you value most in yourself.

Which of these roles do you enjoy most?

What types of rewards are most meaningful to you: money, power, influence, fun, status, recognition, opportunity to grow or learn, challenge, opportunity for more responsibility, opportunity to help others, freedom, etc.?

Meta-Skill Builder 20:
Clarifying Your Purpose

Here is an activity to help you clarify your purpose. Again, read the questions, and then write your answers.

What stories have you heard told about yourself, or do you tell others about yourself, that you enjoy hearing or telling? Make a list of all the tales you have heard told about you. Add to this the stories you have told, either to others or yourself. Do not limit yourself to just the entertaining stories. Include any story that tells something about who you are.

What do you want from life? Say the first thing that comes into your head without censoring.

What is your life's purpose? You might say something as simple as, "to learn all I can," or "to make the world a better place." Or your response might be more lengthy and descriptive. Use what you have just learned about yourself in the earlier parts of this chapter to answer this question.

Who are your heroes? What people or mythological or film characters have inspired and instructed you? Make a list. Next to each name, note why you chose this person. What quality do they have that you value highly?

Imagine you are witnessing your own funeral. Someone close to you is delivering the eulogy. What does this person say? What would you like to be remembered for after you die?

Meta-Skill Builder 21:
Correlating Values and Actions

Now that you have a clearer sense of your values and purpose, let's do an exercise that reveals how closely your behavior corresponds to your values.

Down the left side of a sheet of paper number from one to twenty. Then, as fast as you can, without censoring and in no particular order, list twenty things you love to do. Sometimes it helps to think of the four seasons of the year and to list what you love in each season.

After you have your twenty, it is time to code your responses.

Place a dollar sign to the left of any item which requires an outlay of at least $20. Place a *P* next to any item which is more enjoyable if done with at least one other person. Place an *A* next to items you prefer doing alone. Put a *5* next to the items that would have been on your list five years ago. Star those items you love to do the most. *Finally, for each item, note the approximate date when you last did it.*

When you have finished, look over your list and reflect on what it is telling you about how closely aligned your values are with your behavior.

After completing these values-clarification exercises, reflect upon what you have learned about your essential values. Is there a theme that runs through your answers to the various questions?

When Ann did these exercises, she was disturbed to find that some of her deepest values were not being expressed in her work life or her home life. She had always felt a sense of joy, lightness, and connectedness to others and the earth when she was either walking, dancing, or in some way moving her body. She was most alive and present when she was in motion. Yet her life was structured around a very sedentary routine. As a personnel administrator for a large government agency and single parent of three teenage girls, she realized her life had gone off course somewhere.

How can I put some movement back into my life? she wondered. All I do is chauffeur the girls, commute three hours every day, and then sit another eight or nine hours at a desk. Something isn't right with this picture. Somewhere on the road to success and security, I lost my self.

This recognition made her very sad. She needed her job because she had a family to support. She couldn't just quit and become a ballroom dance teacher. There was no security in that. And besides, she wasn't an especially talented dancer. She just enjoyed it a lot.

If we look at Ann's emerging dissatisfaction in terms of the eight stages of change, we see her shifting back and forth between an awareness that something needs to change and an attempt to silence her discomfort because of her security fears. Accompanying this ambivalence, she was also mourning the loss of connection with her essential self. She could not shake the profound sense of sadness she felt.

As we observed in Chapter Four, deep feeling plus awareness leads to deep healing. Her sadness was to be a critical ingredient in the recovery of her lost self. It helped to acknowledge the pain of her present situation. This pain was coming from her essence. It was the first real connection to her essence that she had felt in a very long time. Her pain helped her find the road back home.

Had she stifled her feelings out of a need to appear in control, she would never have connected with her essential self, which was crying out in pain. By listening to her feelings, she was taking a first step toward healing the split between her outer self and her inner essence. As she let herself become conscious of her need for a change, a vision emerged of how she could bring an entirely new feeling to her present situation—a sense of joy and lightness. In conversations with friends and quiet reflection, she began to explore options for bringing more movement into her life—without quitting her job or changing her residence. Through such reflection and conversation, she was beginning a new relationship with her essential self. As she began listening to it more, it became more expressive. An inner debate ensued between her need for security and her need to express her essence in her work. Each side had a different opinion about what she should do. She was torn. Which side should she listen to?

Most people do not do very well with such internal conflict. We fear it will never be resolved, so we suppress the conflict entirely. But such an important conflict will not just disappear. It will go underground, into our unconscious mind, and create symptoms of distress—symptoms such as anxiety, depression, insomnia, overindulgence in food or alcohol, overwork, irritability, and the like. Anytime you feel such a symptom, you can bet that your neglected essential self is crying out for attention.

Once you begin listening to its messages, the essential self can be a great help in problem-solving. For Ann, the resolution of her internal battle was a gradual process. First, she uncovered an unconscious, outdated belief that work was supposed to be "a stiff, serious, grown-up thing," that she was not earning her pay if she had a good time or moved around when she was addressing people. After she got some perspective on this belief, she began to explore how she might restructure parts of her day so she could spend more time on her feet instead of her backside.

After considerable inner exploration, she arrived at an innovation that became a win for everyone in the personnel department. The department was under fire from the administration because of the backlog of work that had piled up. There were more orientation interviews and exit interviews to be done than they had the staff to handle. Ann's innovation solved both the department's problem and her own. She set up a series of group meetings, which she led, to handle much of the work that used to be done in one-to-one interviews. As it turned out, employees liked these better, it took a load off the rest of the staff, and she got to do more stand-up-and-move-around teaching. She got rave reviews from the participants in her groups. They said she was "inspiring" and "riveting," even though the subject matter was rather pedestrian. Positive feedback like this helped Ann know that she was on course. This was only the beginning of a long process of transforming her life to express more of her essence, but it got her started.

3. Discover Your Essential Vocation

Over the course of your lifetime, your life's purpose, or *essential vocation,* unfolds as an expression of the essential self.

Most of us are not conscious of our purpose. But it can be discovered in the patterns or recurring themes of our lives.

Marion always had a houseful of people. She loved to give parties and entertain. She was a great storyteller. Whenever she came into a room, people would gather around her. Looking for a pattern or theme in her life, she discovered that she was essentially an *entertainer.* She was good at creating settings where people could have a good time. No matter what else she was doing, whether it was meeting a client or attending her son's soccer game, she was entertaining other people. This is how she expresses her life purpose.

Jeremy loved helping people less fortunate than himself. He discovered that he was an *advocate.* Julie had a gift for working with people's physical problems, even though this was not what she did for a living. She was essentially a *healer.* Issac loved to conduct experiments and test out his theories. He was *a scientist* in everything he did.

Although we may remain unconscious of our essential purpose for much of our lives, when it does become conscious, everything we do from that point on is charged with meaning and enthusiasm —as occurred when Tom Melohn connected with his life purpose.

When you find the essential vocation that underlies much of what you do, this adds to your sense of inner stability. Because your essential vocation is an expression of your essential self, it, too, is relatively stable and consistent throughout your lifetime. It does not change when you change your job, your marital status, or your place of residence. When you can move through life feeling grounded in your essential self, you find crisis, change, and conflict less threatening.

It helps to think of your life's work in terms of an essential vocation instead of a set of job duties, because no matter what happens in your job, you can still be a scientist, a teacher, a leader, or an entertainer. When you connect your sense of security to this deeper, more abiding aspect of your being, it becomes easier to stay responsive to external changes, because you are in touch with the changeless core that is within.

Your essential vocation is your essence in action. The term "essential vocation" makes it clear that your essential work is not necessarily tied to the job that you get paid to do. It may be identical with what you do for a living, but often it isn't. Once you know what it is, you will seek ways of expressing it in everything you do. You may already do this without being aware of it. Being aware that you are expressing your essence as you work can greatly enhance your effectiveness and fulfillment.

Using Intuition to Reveal Your Vocation

The more access you have to your intuition, the easier it will be to discover and express your essential vocation. Your intuition knows what is best for you—like a good parent. It is your inner guide. It is available to be consulted when you have an important decision to make. It is the source of the creative "aha" of scientific discoveries. It is the aspect of your mind that is connected to the group or collective mind. Most of us ignore our intuition most of the time. We tell ourselves that we don't have time, or we don't know how, or that the information we receive is not pragmatic enough.

Your intuition already knows your essential vocation, even if your conscious mind has never conceived of the idea. The intuitive sense is like an oracle that we consult when we need an answer to a problem or question in our lives. When you first start to do this on a regular basis, you may have difficulty distinguishing the voice of the intuition from that of the conditioned self. You may wonder, for example, is the answer I'm getting a true reflection of my essence, or is it wishful thinking, fear, or some other form of self-deception? It takes time and practice to come to trust the information you receive when you listen to your inner voice.

Meta-Skill Builder 22:
Listening to Your Intuition

To connect with your intuition, you must first learn to listen in silence. Read over the following guided imagery a few times. Create a comfortable environment by putting on soothing music, dimming the lights, turning off the phone. Sit or lie comfortably. Close your eyes, and allow your breathing to extend down into your belly. Then visualize yourself in the scene described. If distracting thoughts come into your mind, don't fight these. Simply allow them to pass out of your awareness as easily as they entered.

It is a warm, sunny afternoon, and you are walking alone across an open grassy field. As you stroll along, you notice many beautiful birds flying overhead. It is one of those days that makes you feel good to be alive and lucky to be out in nature with so many of Earth's other creatures. About a quarter of a mile up ahead, the path you are on begins to climb upward into a sparsely wooded area. You are feeling energetic so you look forward to the upward climb. Your mind is empty as you walk. You are simply observing and sensing the world around you. You see the birds and hear their sounds. You smell the scent of the various grasses and flowers. You feel the warm sun on your face and body. As the path ascends into the wooded area, you feel the coolness of the shade and hear your footsteps as they rustle in the fallen leaves. You continue for a few minutes before coming to a gigantic rock jutting out of the side of the hill. As you get closer to the rock, you see on one side of the rock the mouth of a cave that penetrates into the hill. You approach the entrance slowly, as a feeling of anticipation quickens in you. You have a sense that you are about to have an experience that will be very important to your future. Inside the cave, you can see six candles burning. You see in their light the outline of a human figure, someone who appears to be very, very old, yet quite vital and in excellent health. As you approach this old person, you are struck by the brightness of this person's eyes. There is a sort of glow that emanates from the eyes, giving you the sense that this person can see deep inside of you. There is a kindness to the face and eyes that makes you trust this person. It is at this point that you realize that there is a question that has been on your mind, a question you would like to ask this old person. The person seems to know what you are thinking and nods approvingly, so you go ahead and ask your question, "What is my calling in life, my essential vocation?" You wait for the answer, and when it comes you sigh audibly. The answer feels right. You offer your thanks and bid your host goodbye. You exit the cave, return to the wooded area, and continue your journey up the hill.

This exercise opens you to the wisdom about your true calling that is contained in the deeper part of your mind. Using this exercise repeatedly will help you make friends with your intuition. You can ask other questions of the wise old person in addition to the question suggested here. When you do not have time to do the entire process, simply take some time out to focus your attention on your breathing. Closing your eyes at the same time also helps. Even a few minutes of this practice a day can yield noticeable results in terms of an ability to focus the attention and quiet the mind at will. When the mind is free of distracting thoughts, the truth rises up into consciousness.

Attracting What You Want

When you hold the vision that your essential self can find expression via your essential vocation, you naturally begin to seek ways of bringing more of yourself to work.

Meta-Skill Builder 23:
Visualizing What You Really Want

A first step in this process is to ask yourself, If I could do any type of work in any type of setting I wanted, what would it be? What would I want? What values would I wish to live by? Then relax, breathe deeply, and create an image in your mind of yourself having exactly what you want.

By creating a positive vision of having what you want, you are revising your image of yourself. A more hopeful self-image creates a container or structure that attracts to it experiences and resources that are consistent with that goal.

Next look for places in your current work life where your essential vocation might find expression. Look especially into areas that have been affected by recent social or organizational changes or areas about to undergo change. A situation in flux is usually full of opportunities. There will be needs that have not yet been addressed, and it is in these areas where your talents might be useful.

Making the Most of Unwanted Changes

Even if you experience a change that makes it harder to express yourself through your work, you are still at an advantage if you already know your essential purpose.

Jerry lost his paramedic job and was transferred to management in another area of city government. He was a big, physically strong man, but he was also very sensitive to the pain of others, very compassionate. Without his paramedic job, he felt truly lost for a while. He saw himself as essentially a *nurturer,* so a lot of his identity had been centered around offering assistance to people in pain.

In his new post, he supervised fifteen employees. As he got to know these people, he realized that his essential talents would still be useful in this new post. He had to look a little harder, and he had to modify his approach, but his *nurturer* became a real asset in his management role. His employees could feel his caring, even though he did not express it directly. And he knew they felt it, which satisfied his need for self-expression. In a few months, Jerry was the acknowledged leader of the most cohesive and productive group in the department.

Meta-Skill Builder 24:
Making the Best of a Bad Situation

Imagine that the worst has happened: due to forces beyond your control, you have been forced to take on a work assignment that feels about as foreign to you as you can imagine. Think of a specific hypothetical worst-case scenario. For example, maybe you are an engineer, and you have been forced to join the sales force. Now think of some way that you might still be able to express your essential vocation in this new position. Be fanciful. Do not worry about whether your thoughts are realistic. But do come up with some ideas about how you might still do what you do no matter what other people think you are doing.

Self-Expression and Company Goals

When the job you get paid to do allows for the expression of your essential self, there is a juiciness to what you do. Your feelings, thoughts, and actions are all of a piece. They feel integrated. When there is only a tiny piece of your essence that can find expression in your job, you feel less than fully alive. But this is better than nothing. To the extent that you can bring at least some of your essence into your regular job, to that extent you will feel emotionally and spiritually connected to your work. Work really can be a source of self-expression and renewal.

W. Edwards Deming, father of the Total Quality movement, spoke passionately about the changes American businesses need to make in order to stay competitive. In his famous "Fourteen Points," he emphasized that extrinsic rewards (like money and status) are no longer enough for American workers. Today's workers need to receive intrinsic rewards from their work. We need to derive a sense of purpose and meaning from what we do. We need to feel that what we do matters—that it has personal significance and significance to the human community. We need work that allows for some measure of authentic self-expression. Nowadays work doesn't just affect our standard of living. It also affects our self-esteem and sense of worth.

Deming traveled all over the world urging companies to change their corporate cultures to reflect these changing trends. As organizations move in this direction, we may see increasing opportunities for bringing our essential selves to work. This will be a blessing if we have taken the time to discover those aspects of ourselves that we wish to nourish and develop through our work. We will then be in good position to discuss with our employers ways to meet personal needs and serve company goals at the same time.

If you have scanned your current work situation and are having difficulty picturing how to employ your essential vocation, ask yourself these questions:

- What is blocking me from expressing my essential vocation here?
- What am I afraid of?
- What am I holding on to?
- What beliefs or assumptions do I have about what is and is not acceptable or useful here?
- Where do these beliefs and assumptions come from?
- What can I learn from this situation even if nothing changes?

If you live for a while with your vision, holding these questions alongside your vision, and you still cannot find an avenue for your essential self, then you may want to consider other employment. But remember, in any job you can be learning about yourself—as long as you do not go into denial and lose connection with your essence.

No matter what your essential vocation, you were still born to learn. Thus, you can always focus on that essential life task, even when other forms of self-expression are not supported by your environment. The simple act of *paying attention* is the essence of inner development work. This is the way to self-knowledge and self-mastery. Whenever you focus your attention totally on the thing you are doing, you learn a tremendous amount about yourself.

In the new workplace, your job is no longer a set of duties and responsibilities. It is more useful to think of your job as "work that needs to be done," or a "mission that needs to be accomplished." Usually, there are a variety of ways to achieve this mission, which might involve using a variety of your talents. The work that needs doing keeps changing, so if you cannot find a way to express your essence in your work today, tomorrow might bring a different situation.

Any organizational system has certain norms and rigidities that you will come up against when you try something new. Do not expect the system to welcome your innovations with open arms. Systems are slow to adapt. The bigger the system, the slower it changes. Instead of taking the resistance you meet personally, see if you can reframe it as information about what fears or cautions exist in the system (or in your supervisor). Then use this information to do what you can to reduce the fear by addressing it and showing how your proposed change will not negatively affect this person or organization. If possible, show how your proposal will actually reduce the likelihood of the feared outcome.

Chapter Ten looks at how to assess the culture of your organization and how to work within that culture for positive change.

If you feel you have done everything you can to bring more of yourself into your job, and this still isn't enough, and you decide to leave your current job, you will need to make a plan for changing jobs. You might use the gap exercise on page 75 to assess all the factors in your present situation. Create a plan that begins by removing the stumbling blocks in yourself and your organization. Then determine specific doable steps for using the stepping-stones to help you achieve your goal. Put these steps in a list with projected dates of completion next to each item. And be prepared to deal with the eight stages of change.

In times of great economic uncertainty, it is more important than ever to do the work necessary to connect with your essential self. In the new workplace, you need to be able to learn quickly, trusting yourself to deal with the unexpected. With so much happening all at once, you need some constant point to focus on—an inner organizing principle to help you find stability and clarity.

One of the great lessons that human civilization is being called to learn in these times is to put more of our energy into *eternals,* like making ourselves, over *externals,* like making a living. When we focus on those things that help us gain a sense of being in control of ourselves, we will not waste energy attempting to control the largely uncontrollable external world.

How Focusing on Your Essential Self Can Make You Indispensable to Your Organization and Customers

1. When you are attuned to your own deeper purpose, you will be more able to assist your organization in discovering and expressing its deepest reason for being. Like individuals, every organization has a unique role to play in the global marketplace. Many organizations, in their attempts to diversify, have lost touch with their original or deeper purpose. In these times of niche marketing, we are seeing how important it is for an organization to stay connected to its unique contribution.

2. In an American Management Association-sponsored investigation into the characteristics employees look for and admire in their leaders, 83 percent of the managers polled selected "honesty" as most important. Internal studies at AT&T and several other organizations have corroborated this finding. These studies emphasize the importance of congruence between words and deeds, values and actions—between a leader's being and doing. When your work is an expression of your essential purpose or values, your behavior comes across as all of a piece. This evokes confidence and trust from your employees and coworkers. In researching the book *The Leadership Challenge,* James Kouzes and Barry Posner found that management's credibility was a major element in enabling others to take action. When employees see their leaders as credible, they are more willing to take risks and move into the unknown without guarantees. If developing employees' self-management capabilities is important in your organization, people must see their leaders behaving congruently.

3. In the new workplace, you need to become a leader, in the best sense of that word, even if you are not in a formal leadership position. You need to be as committed to team and company goals as management is, and you need to be self-managing and self-starting. When you have done the personal self-knowledge work described in this chapter, you are better equipped to align your personal goals with those of the larger system (organization, customer base) that you are serving.

How Focusing on Your Essential Self Can Help You Prevent or Respond to Crisis

1. As cultural values shift in response to world crises (be they economic, geological, political, or currently unimaginable), you will be better able to find a place for yourself in the new order (and even to help shape it) if you are guided by eternal values rather than primarily materialistic values.

2. To deal with potentially overwhelming information and options, it is necessary to know where you stand. Otherwise, you will be blown off course by every strong wind that comes along, thus losing your ability to think clearly and act calmly. Knowing what you value and what you are committed to can help you stay centered in the face of information overload. The ability to focus on what is essential helps you manage potential distractions and know what is worthy of your attention.

And Remember...

- Much of your behavior is governed by learned behavior patterns and beliefs that limit your effectiveness. This set of patterns is called the conditioned self. The Learning/Discovery journey involves recognizing and reevaluating these self-limiting habits.

- You have an essential self that longs to express itself—to give back to the world from what you have been given. Your essential vocation is an expression of your essence. Even in the most rigid work environment, there is usually some avenue for expressing it.

- When your essence has become buried by layers of fears, shoulds, and oughts, you can uncover it by listening to yourself in silence.

CHAPTER SEVEN

Communicate to Build Trust

*To build trusting relationships, we need to communicate with the
intent to learn from others, not to control them. Trust is the glue
that makes effective collaboration and teamwork possible. Without
trust, people become competitive or defensive, and communication
is distorted and unreliable.*

Have you ever found yourself counting on someone else to do
their job so that you could do your job? In the new workplace,
people are highly interdependent. So you need to know you can
trust your coworkers to deliver on their commitments.

Mary was facing a tight deadline. She would win a big contract
for the company if her team performed on time. She heard there
would be a promotion for her if this one went through without a
hitch. But at the eleventh hour, one of her key players, Raymond,
informed her that he would not be able to complete his part of the
project until next week—and he had promised it would be done
yesterday! "How could this be happening to me?" Mary wondered,
seething with anger. Then she remembered: "Raymond tends to
promise more than he can deliver; and he had shown some reluctance when I gave him that assignment. When he agreed to do it,
he was looking around at the piles of paper on his desk, as if to say,
'How could you load more work on me? I'm already overbur-
dened?' He never did look me straight in the eye and commit to
the time frame. I had to extract agreement after some cajoling. His
lips were saying yes, but his insides were saying no. Raymond was
afraid to tell the truth, so he told me what I wanted to hear. Now I

am responsible for his inability to perform. I'm the manager. I'm supposed to know how to get work done through people. I'm in trouble!

"Why did Raymond do this to me?" Mary thought. "I'm not so scary—I could have found a way to work with his time constraints." Perhaps she could have, but Mary did put pressure on Raymond with her impatient attitude. She knew that Raymond tends to be a people-pleaser and hates to disappoint anyone; but she had overlooked that fact because of the pressure she was feeling.

Apparently, Raymond did not feel safe enough to tell Mary the truth. If he had trusted that Mary really wanted to hear his reservations about the project, his response to her request probably would have been quite different.

The presence or absence of trust determines the validity of the communications we receive. Trust creates a feeling of safety—the safety to be honest. To create trusting relationships, we need to communicate with the aim of learning, or mutual understanding, not control. When people feel there is only one "right" answer to your request, they often feel controlled, disrespected, and mistrustful. They may then revert to such protective communication patterns as telling you what you want to hear instead of telling it like it is.

According to a recent study by the Accountemps Personnel Agency, the average company employee spends the equivalent of two months out of every year dealing with problems caused by their own or others' distorted communication patterns. Distorted communication patterns spring from the desire to protect ourselves from something we fear. In Raymond's case, it was his fear of displeasing the team leader. When there is tension in the air, and people feel unsafe being authentic or truthful, they often protect themselves by holding back or distorting information. If our fears were not being triggered, we would not need to protect ourselves.

In the new workplace, your own and your company's success depends upon your being a clear channel for sending and receiving knowledge and information. If you are trying to pressure or control people, they will mistrust you, and you will not get straight communication.

Let's look at how fear blocks authentic communication.

Imagine that someone dares you to walk a fifteen-foot four-by-four-inch beam propped between the ground-floor windows of two adjacent buildings. This would mean the plank would be about five feet off the ground. You would probably rise easily to this challenge and accomplish the feat successfully and confidently.

But let that four-by-four be raised to the fifth story, about fifty feet up, and now your attitude about the walk changes dramatically. Your emotions are instinctively triggered as visions of catastrophic injury or death dominate your awareness. Walking this plank, your movements would be stiff, self-conscious, and tentative.

Put a safety net under you, and again you become more relaxed and agile. Put the four-by-four directly onto the ground, and the walk carries no interest at all.

Objectively, it takes the same degree of skill and agility to walk the plank on the ground, at five feet, or at fifty feet. But subjectively, the experience is entirely different. From the first floor, you enjoyed the novelty and the challenge. One the ground, there was no challenge and therefore not much interest. But from the fifth floor, all you can think of is the possibility of getting hurt. Your attention is dominated by fear.

What does this scenario have to do with communicating to build trust? As we know, people learn and perform best when they are optimally challenged and involved. They learn and perform least well when they are riddled with fear. Thus, it is our job to help the people we interact with feel engaged and challenged, but not deathly afraid.

If someone like Raymond perceives that telling you the truth is equivalent to walking a four-by-four at fifty feet above the ground, he'll be so scared he can't think clearly. He will most likely resort to his habitual self-protective communication pattern—promising with no realistic chance of delivering.

If, on the other hand, he perceives telling you the truth to be a more moderate risk or none at all, because he perceives you as open and respectful rather than controlling, you will probably get the information you need.

Can you think of situations in your life where others' communication appears to be more self-protective than informative? Perhaps they have perceived your relationship as a "fifth-story interaction." Is it possible that their habitual protective patterns are being activated by something you are doing?

Alfred is president of a biomedical research company. At work, he is accustomed to telling people what he wants done and having them do it without question. He doesn't trust his employees very much, and he doesn't expect much trust from them. The job gets done, and that's all Alfred cares about. There is an atmosphere of wariness around his small company, but Alfred has gotten used to it.

Alfred has joint custody of his eleven-year-old son, Nick. At home, Alfred expects a different atmosphere to prevail. Since he only sees his beloved son three days a week, he wants their time together to be quality time. But the two get into problems when it comes time to help Nick with his homework. Alfred is extremely time-conscious and results-oriented. He expects to show Nick how to do something and have Nick "just do what I say." Unfortunately, that is not the way the boy's mind operates. Nick needs a lot of time to think about and question why things are done a certain way. Alfred interprets Nick's questions as insults to his authority. "I know what I'm talking about, Nick! Why do you ask so many questions? You're wasting time!"

Nick becomes sullen and withdrawn when this occurs. He feels misunderstood and disrespected. Alfred, too, feels misunderstood. He is doing his best to help his son, and he gets no acknowledgment. "Home feels frighteningly similar to work," Alfred muses. "Is it them, or is it me?"

Alfred always manages to get the job done, but he lacks the ability to build empowering work relationships. He thinks you just tell someone to do something, and maybe tell them how to do it, and then wait for the results to pour in. His son is teaching him how relationships really work, both at home and at the lab. His son is teaching him about trust and about what happens when it is missing.

Trust is the unseen factor that binds individuals into a high-performing unit. To get a job done effectively, first develop trust and then get down to the task. The process of establishing trust between Alfred and his son would involve their respectfully learning about each other's way of doing things.

When people work together at a common task, we can't assume that trust is automatically present. We must commit to building it through listening, through being honest, and through honoring differences.

When we sense that another person respects our ideas and ways of doing things and wishes to know and understand us, we feel trust. We find it easier to communicate openly with this person. As our own communication becomes more open, this furthers the other's trust. When we trust each other, we have more energy and enthusiasm for working toward shared goals. We are more thorough in exploring the pros and cons of each other's ideas. We are usually more willing to take risks and try new things.

Trust makes mutual learning possible. That is why it is so critical in today's learning organization, which is founded upon cooperative problem-solving, team creativity, and alliances of mutual benefit.

Mistrust creates fear. When we sense that another person is trying to control us or get us to do or see things his way, we feel wary and protective. The need to control others kills trust. As we saw with Alfred and his son Nick, it also kills your ability to work effectively as a team.

Trust is based on two-way, as opposed to one-way, communication. When someone orders us to do something, without regard to whether this makes sense to us, we feel disrespected and therefore resistant. When our input is considered, we feel respected and therefore more trusting.

This does not mean that all relationships must be egalitarian and nonhierarchical. Trust can flourish in a supervisory relationship if the supervisor expresses himself with the intent of mutual understanding. A manager or supervisor can retain his areas of control and still be open to learning from other people.

An effective leader values all inputs, recognizing that he alone cannot know all there is to know. He may still be the final authority on the matter, but this need not make people feel controlled. People feel controlled when they feel their point of view is not considered.

Sometimes, if a disagreement between supervisor and supervisee cannot be resolved, it is important that the supervisor spell out the probable consequences of acting contrary to his recommendations.

This can be done in a way that still gives the employee a choice, without threatening the employee. If the employee does not follow the supervisor's guidance, there may be certain consequences. But the supervisor does not become emotionally punitive or take the employee's actions personally.

Meta-Skill Builder 25:
Reflecting on Your Own Experiences

Recall an occasion when you and another person or group were able to accomplish something of outstanding value together. What were the ingredients that made this joint effort so successful? Did trust have anything to do with it?

Was the leader focused on controlling people or on including and learning from their ideas?

How did the leader's behavior affect the way people communicated with one another?

Did people listen to and respect everyone's contribution?

What specifically did the leader do that helped to build trust?

Now recall a time when you were not able to work together effectively with others.

What did each of you specifically do that revealed the presence of fear or mistrust? Did you see any evidence of self-protective communication patterns?

What might people have been afraid of?

What did the leader do or not do that contributed to fear and lack of trust?

What did others do that also contributed to lack of trust?

Let me tell you about a "fifth-story" (high-stakes) relationship in my life, and how my fear of the other person seriously distorted our capacity for collaborative problem-solving. This person was my father.

When I was about ten, I was always uneasy in my father's presence. I didn't know why he affected me this way. I thought maybe it was his booming voice, or the fact that, since we rarely communicated, I never knew what he was thinking. All I knew was that I couldn't do anything right around him.

My family home had an old barnlike structure out back, which my parents allowed me to use as my playhouse. It had been designed as a carpentry workshop. There was a workbench and a place for tools; but since my father wasn't a handyman, I got to use it instead as my retreat from the adults.

I called it "The Becker Street Playhouse." It was my own little neighborhood theater where I put on circuses, plays, and magic shows for my younger brothers and their friends.

One day, as I was planning my next magic show, I got a brilliant idea—or so it seemed at the time. My parents had just given me their old dining-room set so I could upgrade the furnishings in the playhouse. I would use the dining-room table to display my props, and the chairs to seat my audience. And then there was this old sideboard. What could I do with that?

As I opened its double doors, I realized that I could fit my entire little body inside this piece of furniture. This led to my brilliant idea. I could remove the back and tack a tan-colored drape over the opening. Then I would cut a hole in the floor right behind it, so I could easily slip out the back, and drop down into the basement —a drop of about five feet. As the grand finale of my magic show, I would do a disappearing act! I would say some magic words, climb into the sideboard, and deftly disappear, a moment later to reappear at the rear of the room near the basement stairs! I performed this feat of magic many times to the continued amazement of the neighborhood children.

One day, my father decided to come out to the workshop to have a look around. He still thought of it as his workshop even though I'd actually done a lot more carpentry out there than he ever had—like sawing out those floorboards and replacing them with a thin, easily removable piece of particle board. He looked around my playhouse with a frown. "I don't like how you have the furniture arranged," he announced. (I had placed the sideboard in the center of the room, to cover the hole in the floor.) "This should be up against a wall," he said as he stepped toward the sideboard.

At that point, I had a decision to make—should I warn him or just hope for the best? As I debated this question, my decision got made for me. He lifted the sideboard off the hole, stepped on that thin piece of particle board, and disappeared into the basement!

My fear of speaking up to my father really got me into trouble.

Actually, it got us both into trouble. I lost the privilege of using the workshop as my playhouse, and he got some scrapes and bruises.

The story has two morals—one for employees and one for managers. First, as the employee, when you let fear get in the way of honest communication, you lose your power to create magic. And second, as a manager, if people are afraid to tell you the truth, you might wind up in the basement like my father!

Using this story as a backdrop, I'd like to look further at the costs of lack of trust in relationships, where the accurate exchange of information is vitally necessary.

Like many managers and supervisors, my dad had no idea that I was afraid of him. As it turns out, he had his own areas of insecurity. Why would anyone fear him? And like many employees in relation to their supervisors, I saw my dad as much more powerful than he really was. If I had felt more trusting, I might have sought his support in making a better trapdoor through which to disappear. In my fear state, I could not imagine how he might join me or support my efforts; but in retrospect, I see that he might have been quite helpful.

Can you see how my fears prevented me from enlisting his help to build a better trapdoor?

These fears were not completely unfounded, however. I had gotten the message from my father on more than one occasion that he would rather control me than listen to me. I may have overgeneralized my mistrust, but his manner was partly responsible for my fear of communicating openly with him.

Fear shuts off the information flow so vital to cooperative problem-solving. As a child, I felt invalidated when my father sought his privacy by ignoring me or when he tried to get me to agree with him by dominating the conversation. I got the message that his intent was to control me, not to learn with me. So I did what most kids would do—I kept a lot of secrets from him. I learned to hold back my feelings, ideas, and observations.

As a manager, when you send the message that your intent is to control, others tend to hide their true feelings and thoughts from you. When you communicate that your intent is mutual understanding, *to know and be known,* vital information becomes available to you.

All communication either builds trust or weakens it. Everything you say, do, or feel toward another has an intention behind it. People always sense whether your intent is to understand or to control. When it is to control, they feel used, disrespected, invalidated. The relationship is limited. You lose the ability to solve problems together or to contribute to one another's learning.

In the new learning-oriented workplace, the critical competitive raw material is peoples' knowledge and their ability to cocreate knowledge through free and open exchanges with one another. A healthy system (person, partnership, team, organization) is one characterized by the free exchange of energy, information, and feelings. This requires trust.

Driving Fear Out

Because work gets done through people, and people need good communication in order to get their work done, the new workplace demands a new order of people skills. Nine of W. E. Deming's famous "Fourteen Points" of Total Quality Management are about the importance of interpersonal feelings and relationships in the workplace.

In *Out of the Crisis,* Deming sees fear as the most significant barrier to quality, productivity, and innovation. In his overview of the types of fears people typically report, he lists job loss, poor performance ratings, limited career options, loss of personal credibility, and lack of trust of management. In his writings and lectures, Deming challenges American companies to "drive fear out" of the workplace.

According to Deming, "the fundamental problem in American business is that people are scared to discuss the problems of people." The reason for this lack of trust relates to the very fears Deming lists—fears of job loss, of losing face, and so forth.

We see a vicious cycle here: we are in a fear state because we may lose our job, our credibility, etc. This makes us unwilling to take the risk of openly discussing our people problems. If we were not so afraid, we would be having these discussions. We would be working together to address the causes of our fears—and possibly

eliminating these causes—but we can't get there from here because we are too afraid of the repercussions of initiating these
discussions.

In their recent book, *Driving Fear Out of the Workplace,* based
on interviews with 260 employees in a broad spectrum of organizations, Kathleen Ryan and Daniel Oestreich report that employees
tend to avoid discussing problems directly with the person responsible for the problem. In other words, when there is a problem, we
do not communicate with the people who can help us solve it. We
talk about it behind their backs, or we resort to various impersonal
grievance procedures.

The tendency to avoid conflict is the result of a deep and perva-
sive vein of mistrust in the system. This limits the effectiveness of
our working relationships and costs our companies millions of dollars in expenses for litigation, unions, disability, sick leave, and the
like.

As we saw in Chapter Six, fear originates in the conditioned layer
of the human personality. This "fear layer" is often covered by a
layer of denial: "I'm okay. Everything's gonna be all right." This
mask is but a thin veneer, however. When something goes wrong
in the external world, which is where most peoples' self-worth is
founded, an emotional reaction is triggered that breaks through the
surface politeness.

We all harbor unacknowledged fears and automatic self-protective reactions. We have "buttons" that get pushed when we feel
threatened. Most people have an automatic negative reaction to
being controlled or criticized. When our criticism or control buttons get triggered, we instinctively defend or attack in an effort to
protect ourselves.

To eliminate fear from our relationships so that work can proceed smoothly, we must learn to communicate respectfully, even
if we passionately disagree with someone.

Respectful communication has these five vital qualities:

1. It seeks to know and be known. It is based on the intent to learn
   about the other and to have the other know us.
2. It is honest and encourages honesty.
3. It honors the other's right to have his own point of view, which
   may be different from our own.

4. It shows empathy for the other's feelings.
5. It seeks common ground. It focuses on areas of agreement or commonality as a basis for exploring areas of disagreement.

1. Respectful Communication Is Based on the Intent to Learn

The most powerful aspect of communication is intent. Intent is the unspoken message in the message. Although rarely acknowledged directly, it tells the other person what we want. Our intent is always received.

Here is a statement that might seem like a simple sharing of one's feelings: "It upsets me when you agree to something and then don't follow through. I get disappointed and feel you don't care about me." If your intent was to get the other to change to make you feel better, and you are unaware of this, you may be shocked when others do not respond as expected. Your sharing may sound like a simple plea to know and be known, but on closer examination, it may be based on the intent to control.

The intent of any communication will generally fall into one of two categories: wanting something from the other; or wanting to learn.

When we tell someone what we are feeling, we may want them to change their behavior by making them feel sorry, guilty, or responsible for us, or we may want help in clarifying our feelings or thoughts.

When our intent is to control, others will sense this and are likely to become defensive, passively resistant, or overly solicitous. The attempt to control people always backfires. They may comply for a while, but in the longer term, they become less open to our influence—because they do not trust us.

The intent to learn about and with the other creates a sense of shared exploration and discovery. Trust, creativity, and synergy are the results.

Meta-Skill Builder 26:
Receiving Negative Feedback

Think of a person you know who has a high need to control other people. Imagine that this person is giving you feedback on an important piece of work you have just completed. And imagine that this other person is not entirely pleased with what you have done. Write an imaginary dialogue of the conversation between you and this person, including your responses to this person's feedback.

Now think of a person who is more open, with little need to control others. Imagine that this person is giving you feedback on that same piece of work, and imagine that this person, too, is not entirely pleased. Write both parts of this dialogue, the other's feedback and your response.

How different is your response to each of these people? Are you more open to the person who is more open to learning from and about you? What are some of the subtler aspects of this more open person's behavior as compared with the subtler aspects of the more control-oriented person? Are the results of these two approaches significantly different?

2. Respectful Communication Is Honest

Remember Raymond in the beginning of this chapter? He didn't feel safe enough to tell his team leader that he could not meet the requested deadline. Remember how my dad fell through the hole in the floor because I couldn't be honest with him?

What prevents us from being honest? Why are we so afraid to talk straight to each other? Most fears, as we have seen, are fears of loss. We fear we will lose approval, power, acceptance, status, face, money, comfort, a job, an opportunity, credibility, and the like. These are things no one wants to lose.

On the other hand, what are the consequences of being dishonest in order to protect ourselves from possible loss? Tom Melohn told me that when he was the CEO of North American Tool & Die, he would not tolerate dishonesty of any type. "One day, an employee tried to cover up a mistake instead of admitting it and learning from it. Everyone knew he was covering up," states Melohn. "This man lost more respect and credibility from his peers and superiors on that day than he could ever have imagined. I would have respected him if he had come to me and said, 'I know I was in error here. What can I do to make amends?' "

How Honesty Gets Distorted

Psychologists have found that unresolved past emotional incidents have subtle but profound effects on the adult communication patterns. An unfinished situation exists in your mind when you don't get a chance to say what you feel or stand up for yourself. Unfinished situations can exert a powerful internal force, creating events that are mysteriously similar to those forgotten incidents that happened in childhood. If you could not get your father's respect as a child, for example, you may have difficulty being honest around male authority figures because you need their approval so much. Or if your mother was critical of you as a child, you may find yourself unable to express yourself in the presence of women who appear critical.

Not long ago, I was doing some management coaching with Terrance, a thirty-five-year-old sales manager employed by a major clothing manufacturer. His story illustrates dramatically how an unfounded fear, learned at an early age, can distort one's communication from that point forward.

Terrance's boss, the district sales manager, had set up a series of performance coaching sessions for Terrance because of Terrance's convoluted communication style. He became defensive whenever anyone asked him a direct question. He was not able to give clear, direct answers to questions from customers or coworkers.

He confessed to me that he had the same problem at home. His wife complained that if she asked him a simple, nonaccusing question like "Did you water the garden today?" Terrance would get tense and tongue-tied and start making excuses: "I had to get the oil changed in my car . . . and then my computer printer broke down . . . and my boss needed me to travel to Buffalo . . ."

At work, the pattern was the same. One day, his manager called him in for a conference: "Hey, Terrance, I notice you haven't been calling on the O'Toole account lately. How come?" Terrance flushed and nearly stammered his reply: "Oh, that Richard O'Toole really lacks class. You should see the office furniture he just bought —really gaudy and tasteless. And he spends more time at the gym than at the office. I don't know about that guy...." Terrance was unaware of his manager's quizzical expression. And he had no idea how much his defensiveness was costing him, careerwise, until his manager recommended the coaching sessions.

Let's look at how Terrance became aware of the roots of his defensive communication pattern. He readily admitted he'd always been uncomfortable with any direct questioning, but he had no idea where the pattern might have originated.

After he got comfortable talking about himself with me, more and more memories from his childhood began to surface. He recalled numerous instances when he was encouraged to tell the truth in response to direct questioning from his mother. When he did so, he was immediately punished. So he developed the self-limiting belief and fear that it isn't safe to be honest, especially in response to direct questioning. It soon became clear that this belief was a major factor in creating his present defensiveness in responding to direct questions.

He told me that now, when anyone asks him a question, "It's as if there's a small, scared voice inside me, like the voice of a child saying, 'Don't answer that. It's not safe. Watch out.' "

After discovering the outdated belief that he would get punished if he answered directly and truthfully, Terrance decided to take a risk and test out this belief. He began, first with his wife and later with the people at work, to pause and think every time he was asked a question. He created for himself a mental-emotional reminder: any time he was asked a question, he would silently say to himself, "Let me pause to decide how to answer that question." This was his wake-up signal to stop acting automatically defensive and begin to really choose his answers.

In less than a year, he had almost completely outgrown his lifelong habit of defensiveness. He still heard that little scared voice in his head when he was asked a question, but his new habit of pausing to choose his response gave him the opportunity to remind himself, that was then, and this is now. His wife was overjoyed. His manager was amazed.

Meta-Skill Builder 27: Your "Honesty Story"

Reflect on your own "honesty story," noting when, where, and what you learned. Try to step out of the story, viewing it as an objective observer might. See if you can discover any beliefs that you acquired from this story. Do these beliefs still seem valid today? Do they need to be updated or revised?

Usually, the rules we made up to protect us from being hurt as children are no longer needed now that we are grown up. But we often forget to revise them. Take some time right now to update yours. If you need help, go back and review the X-Ray Process on page 114.

Meta-Skill Builder 28:
Your Fears and Beliefs About Honesty

Here is an activity to help you learn about your fears of being honest. Ask yourself:

In what types of situations am I wary of telling the truth? (Check those that apply to you.)

_____contract negotiations
_____sales negotiations
_____other types of negotiations
_____when I know the other(s) will be upset with me
_____receiving unrealistic assignment or an assignment I may not be successful at
_____receiving negative feedback
_____reporting project performance to management
_____responding to questions from children
_____responding to questions from spouse (note types of questions)
_____delivering performance reviews
_____delivering bad news to management
_____responding to customer complaints
_____giving feedback to peers
_____giving feedback to boss or other superiors
_____giving feedback to supervisees
_____any situation where the other has power over me

_____any situation where I feel I need the other's approval
_____other situations

As you look at the types of situations that make you wary (above), what is your specific fear of loss in each case? Note the fear for each situation you checked off. Now ask:

1. What is the belief that supports this fear?
2. When have I felt this fear before?
3. What happened to me in the past to reinforce this fear?
4. When is the first time I can recall feeling this fear?
5. How did I put it together in my mind that honesty was con- nected to this feared outcome? (Again, reviewing the X-Ray Process can be helpful.)

Are Others Honest with You?

Do people feel they can be honest with you? Here's how you can tell: Think of a specific ongoing relationship in your life. Now look back over your interactions with this person in the past year or two, and note how often you heard (a) bad news, (b) good news, (c) no news, (d) their reactions or feelings about something you did. If you heard only good news or no news (e.g., small talk), you and this person may have a communication problem. Maybe this person is afraid of you. Maybe she cares too much about what you think or what you could do to her. Maybe she thinks you don't care or don't want to know.

Here is a story that illustrates the importance of maintaining respectful communication with your coworkers. At a certain city post office, no one liked the day-shift supervisor, Jane. Jane was one of those people who reprimanded you and punished you by giving you less desirable jobs if you called attention to things that were not going well. She seemed unable to cope with bad news of any type. So her employees decided not to inform her when things weren't proceeding according to plan. "If she wants to think there are no problems around here, we'll let her," they decided.

In the post office, there are important jobs that have to be done at specific times so that each piece of equipment is available when needed and so that certain types of parcels are ready when pickup time comes. Unbeknownst to Jane, for over a week no one was at a particular critical work station from 11 A.M. to noon, which was just the time these parcels needed to be sorted so they would get out on time.

All of her employees knew that this station was vacant and that the work wasn't getting done, but no one bothered to inform Jane. It was her job to tell people which job to do, and if she didn't specifically tell someone to be somewhere, they acted as if they didn't know. So the workers just watched with a certain glee as they waited for her to get into trouble with her boss for overlooking a problem that would certainly slow down operations not only at this postal site but also at several others down the line. Pretty soon, Jane would see where her "Don't rock the boat" style of management had led. If you punish people for telling you what's going on, pretty soon they stop informing you.

If people aren't talking to you as much as they used to, you may want to ask, "How well am I listening? Am I open to all types of information—even bad news or information about how I'm perceived? And do I ever unwittingly blame the messenger?"

The postal workers in Jane's office felt they would be punished for being honest. In the past, their efforts to be helpful had been met with disrespect. So now they withhold their potentially helpful knowledge. When we hide or cover up, we damage our relationships and destroy the possibility for mutual learning. If learning is the basis for success in the new workplace, we must help each other feel safe to be honest.

3. Respectful Communication Honors Differing Viewpoints

In a world of increasing diversity, you need to know how to learn from people who don't speak your language—to approach people who see things differently than you do with a sincere intent to learn about their vantage point.

In Security/Control, you feel as if your personality habits and beliefs are who you are, so that if you should change a habit or a belief, it feels as if you have lost or compromised something of yourself. It's easy to forget that your habits and views are not who you really are. They are usually based on your conditioning, not on your essence.

In Learning/Discovery, you know that changing your habits and perceptions does not change your essence. You value the learning that comes from shifting perspectives. When you make it a priority to honor different viewpoints, your people problems significantly decrease. You can build bridges between yourself and others who may initially disagree with you.

Listening Is Honoring

One of the inevitable tensions of life is the tension between self and other, your needs and my needs, your right to autonomy and my desire to influence you. Respectful communication considers both sides of this eternal tension. It is practical and realistic because it does not deny the importance of either the self or the other.

The classic model of respectful communication is, "I think, feel, want _____. What do you think, feel, want?" or "Can you give me this?" or "How does that fit with your wants?" You state your viewpoint or your wish, and invite the other to respond. If she responds affirmatively or agreeably, she has done so voluntarily. She has not been coerced, so she is more apt to really do what she has agreed to do, and to do it wholeheartedly. In respectful communication, you do your very best to get your views and wishes across without infringing on the other person's right to hold a different view.

Loni and Klaus, while working together on a marketing plan, have come to a point of disagreement. Loni wants to hire a market research firm to conduct preliminary studies. Klaus feels this would be a waste of money and time. After listening to Loni's reasons for wanting to do preliminary research, Klaus offers a respectful reply, "Loni, I understand that you feel we need to be clearer on customer needs before we spend all this money on a marketing video. I can see that you want to survey a large sample of customers because you don't like assuming we know their needs. Is that right?" After Loni replies in the affirmative, he continues: "Before we assume that we don't know enough about our customers, I'd like to show you this report that was completed just last month by our competitor. Will you go over it with me to see if it gives us the information we need?"

In offering evidence of his respect, Klaus listened to and considered Loni's idea. While he disagreed with her position, he did not criticize it or put it down in any way. Then he let her know that he had a different approach to the problem. Whatever the outcome, it is probable that the tone set by Klaus will probably continue. This kind of respect allows the pair to learn from one another and to solve problems as a team.

Respect for differences is more an attitude than a technique, but there are certain behaviors associated with it. We communicate respect by listening with our full attention and by reflecting back our understanding of the other's viewpoint. This helps to build trust. As a result, both people are freer from anxiety, defensiveness, fear, and all those other emotions that weaken our ability to be productive and resourceful.

When you are respecting differences, you know that it is not always possible to get what you want. You know that life is a two-way exchange. Remember, all commerce, both social and economic, is based on the principal of *exchange*—giving something and getting something else. The key transaction is, What do I want? and What do you want? Thus, all commerce involves two-way communication.

Interviewing in Order to Learn About the Other

You probably do a great deal of interviewing in the course of a typical day. You ask salespeople and suppliers about their prices and about what kind of a deal you can get. You ask friends and coworkers about their plans. You ask if there is anything they need from you. Most of us take interviewing for granted because it is such an integral, and often unconscious, part of our daily lives.

To renew your appreciation for this time-honored skill, imagine what your life would be like if you were never allowed to ask any questions:

Your customers stop buying your product and turn to your competitor. You have to guess why because you aren't allowed to ask questions. You make some assumptions, you change your product accordingly, you wait to see if your customers come back. Good luck.

Your star salesman, Jake, has three terrible months in a row, when he doesn't even come close to making quota. Other salespeople are doing about the same as usual. You wonder what Jake's problem is. But, of course, you can't ask. So, again, you guess. You do what you can to assist Jake, but nothing changes. Finally, after a few more bad months, Jake quits. You never know why.

As you can see, you'd be in real trouble if you weren't able to gather information from others. But I'm betting that there are many situations in your life where you either act as if you weren't allowed to ask questions, or where you move too quickly into a *telling* mode instead of pausing to gather more information. That is why I like to emphasize the importance of *interviewing* as a prime example of respectful communication. In selling, in parenting, in performance coaching, in leading, in enlisting others' cooperation and help, interviewing is essential.

Meta-Skill Builder 29: Asking Versus Telling

To help you discover situations in your life where you may be *telling* when you should be *asking,* here are some familiar interpersonal situations in which people typically do not gather enough information:

- An employee asks why she didn't get a bigger raise or bonus. Do you simply tell her, or do you also ask what she thought she deserved and why?
- Someone disagrees with your position on an important matter. Do you reassert your position, or do you find out more about why the other person holds the position she does?
- Someone from sales informs you that customers aren't buying your company's hot new product. Do you tell him to be a better salesperson, to think more positively, or do you ask for this salesperson's observations about conditions in the marketplace?
- An employee is doing the minimum amount of work to get by. Do you tell him how his performance must improve, or do you start by asking him what is going on with him?

- People in your section are sending E-mail messages to one another about issues that have come up in staff meetings. They seem to be avoiding face-to-face communication. Do you issue an E-mail message on the subject telling them that this is counterproductive, do you tell them this at the next staff meeting, or do you bring the matter up at the next staff meeting and ask what they think the problem might be?

In completing this checklist, what did you learn about yourself? Did you discover any situations where you were telling when perhaps you should have been asking?

Think of a recent situation where someone was attempting to enlist your help in getting a job done, and where this person told you what to do (and perhaps how to do it) rather than finding out about your ideas or interests? Did you feel respected? How did that affect your enthusiasm for doing this work?

Although most of us have developed some interviewing skill in the course of our lives, here is a list of generic, all-occasion, interview questions that you can use to improve your interviewing. These questions, when delivered with a respectful openness to the other person, often elicit a fairly deep level of information and self-disclosure.

- Could you tell me more about why you see it that way (or think or feel that way)? This question is useful for defusing another's argumentativeness when they are disagreeing with you.
- How does that work, as you see it?
- Why do you say that?
- What are your options? Or, How do you see your options?
- Can you go into that a bit more? Can you explain that further?
- When has that happened before? This question is useful when someone expresses a feared outcome.
- Could you give an example? Could you be more specific?
- Why don't you want to do that? This question can be especially useful when your child or teenager is refusing a request.
- Tell me more about why you don't think that will work.
- How might that be? This question is useful if you really don't understand what the other is talking about enough to ask a more

specific question. It is designed to get the other person to elaborate or clarify.

Interviewing establishes the fact that you are interested in the other person. It helps build trust. This tends to defuse the other's resistance to you because he feels safer, less protective, and more relaxed in your presence. In the process, it also yields important information about the other person, which can be especially useful in problem-solving, customer service, sales, or negotiations.

Interviewing to Get Feedback

Interviewing can also be useful for learning from others how your actions impact them or what you might do to be more effective. When you seek feedback from others, this shows a sincere intent to learn.

Often, if you are in a position of authority, people will not volunteer their observations on your behavior. You need to let them know that you want their feedback. It helps also to let them know what you specifically want feedback on.

How comfortable are you in seeking feedback? Ask yourself these questions:

- What is my overall feeling about hearing how my actions affect others?
- Have I ever asked people how my style or actions have affected them?
- When I ask, do I really want them to tell me the truth?
- Is it okay from superiors but not from subordinates (or the other way around)?
- Do I view it as a part of my job?
- Have I ever really benefited from feedback?
- What am I most interested in hearing about my performance or style?
- Am I better at receiving supportive or critical feedback?
- Do I hear feedback about my performance as a statement about my adequacy as a person? What might I need to learn so that I do not take things so personally? (The X-Ray Process on page 114 addresses this issue.)

When someone gives you feedback *at your request,* this helps to create a bond between you. If his feedback happens to be negative, and you receive it openly, this can have an even more beneficial effect. It can help him let go of the negative feeling or impression he may have been carrying. Thus, feedback is a very important tool for clearing away the emotional baggage that often accumulates in a relationship. The ability to initiate it and the ability to respond openly to it are equally important.

Interviewing to Learn Together

What if you and a coworker have had a satisfying relationship, but then something goes wrong and communications break down? Perhaps one of you feels let down by a broken agreement or lack of effective performance. Maybe one person's feelings have been hurt. Or perhaps neither of you know what caused the problem.

If this should occur, suggest that the two of you sit down together and use a combination of interviewing and active listening to reach understanding on the issue. Start by suggesting that because this relationship is such an important one, and because something seems to be getting in the way of your once-satisfying communication, you'd like to invite the other to explore with you possible reasons for the change in your relationship.

Then one of you begins by telling how you view the matter, while the other *interviews* to draw out more feelings or information and *actively listens,* or reflects back what he has heard, to show that he hears what you are feeling. It is essential that both people get equal time to express themselves and that the purpose of mutual understanding is agreed upon at the start.

The next section on empathy describes more fully how the two communication tools of interviewing and active listening are used together.

4. Respectful Communication Shows Empathy

Empathy is the experience of putting yourself in another's place and seeing the world through her eyes. When you successfully communicate empathy for another, she feels "This person is with me—this person understands me." This helps her feel more trusting and open in your presence.

In showing empathy, it is not necessary to forsake your own point of view if it differs from the other's. You simply hold your viewpoint "off to one side" momentarily while your focus on her feelings or opinions.

The best technique for developing empathy is the active-listening technique of restating the speaker's words and feelings. Listen for what she seems to be feeling, and restate this to see if it is correct. If you cannot pick up on a feeling, then select what seem to be the key words or phrases that capture the sense of her message and restate these. Then ask if you have heard her correctly.

Here is an example of empathic communication using active listening, from a conversation between Thornton and Janice, co-workers in a large manufacturing company:

Thornton stomps over to Janice's desk, looking agitated and upset: "I'm so frustrated. I can't get those guys down in purchasing to do anything for me. They always have one excuse or another why they can't do what I want."

Janice replies empathically, "Sounds like you're really frustrated not getting the cooperation you need."

Feeling Janice's empathy helps Thornton relax a bit before continuing: "Yes, and I've tried talking to their manager, but he doesn't like to rock the boat. I'm at a loss about how to get our orders filled."

Janice stays with him: "And you're feeling stuck. You've talked to their boss. You feel like you've tried everything and don't know where to go next." This reply seems to help Thornton stay focused on the problem.

He appears calmer as he continues: "Maybe I'll have to talk directly to those guys about the problems we're having up here. Maybe if they knew what we were going through, they'd listen."

Janice follows with "So now you're thinking of talking to them directly to give them a better sense of our needs."

Thornton nods and gives her a relieved smile. "Yes, I know what I'm going to do." He walks away with a determined gait and a look of resolution.

As you can see, communicating empathy takes self-discipline. In actively listening to him, Janice did not express agreement or disagreement. Often it is tempting to just agree with someone when trying to show empathy, but this is not as helpful as what she did.

Note, too, that she did not offer advice, which also would have been easier. Instead, she showed Thronton that her attention was on *him,* not on her own needs to give answers or advice. She gave him room to explore and discover his own solution. And she offered just enough comment to give him a feeling of support and help him stay focused. With that minimal amount of reflection, Thornton was able to solve his own problem.

If Janice had done more, Thornton probably would have done less. Empathic communication is empowering. It leaves control in the hands of the speaker and supports him in developing his own resources.

What if Janice, as many of us tend to do, had offered her own opinion and advice instead of empathy? How might Thornton respond then? Let's try it and see.

Thornton starts out as before: "I'm so frustrated. I can't get those guys down in purchasing to do anything for me. They always have some excuse."

But this time Janice replies in a more controlling manner: "Thornton, you need to be more assertive with those guys, you know, more forceful. Let them know that they are here to serve the customer, and we are their internal customers." Her advice might be good, but it suggests that she knows better than he does what he should do. This does not show respect for his ability to handle things in his own way.

Here is one possible way that Thorton might respond to her overly helpful style: "Yeah, I guess so, I could do that. But I don't think it'll do any good." He exits the conversation without any sense of resolution.

People need a skillful listener in times of stress. When met with good advice, most of us would probably reply with something similar to Thornton's "Yeah, I guess so." When their frustrations are met with empathy, they feel more open and trusting. This helps them become more trusting of themselves—of their own inner resources.

People own the solutions they participate in discovering. This makes them more committed to making these solutions work. In the nonempathic example, Thornton felt no ownership for Janice's suggestion. Thus, he doubted that it would work. Empathy is a great help in empowering others to be their responsible and creative best.

Meta-Skill Builder 30:
Active Listening with Difficult People

Think of a person you are having trouble communicating with, and note what it is about this person that puts you off. Now imagine, and then write, an imaginary conversation in which the other person explains to you why she behaves in this irritating way. Imagine and then write what you would say back to this person in response to her explanation. In your response, attempt to show empathy for her feelings and needs using active listening.

5. Respectful Communication Seeks
Common Ground

As we have just seen, active listening is the process of reflecting back to the speaker your sense of what he is feeling. The main purpose of active listening is to let the other know that you are following what he is saying, that you are actively engaged and present to the interaction. Usually, this tool is reserved for fairly serious conversations, where a problem needs to be solved or a conflict reconciled.

In problem-solving, when a person feels actively listened to, he begins to listen more carefully to himself, and as a consequence, he gets clearer on his own feelings. We saw this in the conversation between Janice and Thorton—how we often discover the resources within ourselves to solve our own problems when we feel someone is paying careful attention to us.

In a conflict situation, active listening can serve to establish a sense of common ground. This may lead the other to soften her position. She feels you are already with her so there is less need to resist you. Sometimes in conflict or negotiation situations, active listening can be combined with *interviewing* to search for the interests and feelings underneath the other party's stated position. This builds trust while at the same time providing useful information for discovering common ground.

The negotiations of everyday life offer many opportunities for active listening and interviewing. Tony was director of the technical writing department for a large corporation. Rita was one of his tech writers. One day, Tony invited Rita in to his office to discuss something important. "I want you to start coming in an hour and a half earlier," he told Rita.

Rita was stunned. She knew immediately that she could not do this because coming in earlier would mean she would have to go to bed so early that she would miss her only time to be with her husband and children. She reacted instinctively: "Tony, you know I can't do that. I hardly ever get to see my family as it stands now!" Tony countered threateningly, "Look, Rita, you need to get your priorities straight."

Instantly, Rita could see where this conversation was headed. So she shifted her attitude and remembered how much more relaxed she felt when she was able to take a sincere interest in the other's needs and interests, and how that approach fit better with her Learning/Discovery values. Shifting gears, Rita began to ask Tony some questions: Why was he suggesting this? What were the needs and interests behind his suggestion? And finally, were there any other ways of satisfying these objectives besides having her come in earlier?

This approach, in addition to giving her important data, gave her time to collect herself. In order to show that she understood him, she reflected back to Tony her sense of his needs and interests. From this process, she learned that he wanted her there early because he was grooming her for a management position; that he needed one-on-one time at the beginning of the day because later on he got too busy to concentrate.

As she continued to interview him and understand his interests, it became apparent that there was much common ground between them. They both wanted to have one-on-one time together every day, and they both wanted her to be promoted to manager. Pretty soon the conversation became more like a cooperative problem-solving session and less like a tug-of-war. By the end of the discussion, Tony and Rita had agreed that she would call him every morning from her car phone on the way to work. This would take place early before Tony became inundated with demands. She would not have to get up any earlier, and they would still get the one-on-one time they needed.

Finding common ground, with the help of skillful interviewing and active listening, set the stage for a cooperative exploration of options. If they had not taken the time to establish their common interests, if the conversation had continued as it began, they might have gotten stuck butting heads instead of putting their heads together.

In addition to its considerable value in problem-solving and conflict resolution, the interviewing/active-listening combination can be very helpful when someone is attacking you or blowing off steam in your direction. If you can relax and "fall back" into the active listening mode, perhaps, occasionally asking a nonchallenging, information-seeking question, you will have a chance to get centered, and the other will often relax and cool down. Remember to check your intent: is it to learn what is really troubling this person or to get her to stop what she is doing? You may be surprised at how receptive even very angry people are to a sincere attempt to be understood.

Active listening helps you remain calm while you search for common ground in an intense conflict situation.

Meta-Skill Builder 31: Active Listening in Negotiations

Recall a conflict or negotiation situation you have been in recently where things did not turn out as you would have liked. Replay in your mind as much of the conversation as you can recall. Can you see places where you could have used interviewing or active listening? Rewrite the scene as it might have gone if you had been able to use these two tools successfully.

Preparing the Ground for Feedback

We have just seen how establishing common ground can make communication easier and more productive when two people have differing positions.

COMMUNICATE TO BUILD TRUST • 165

Another use of the common-ground principle is as a preparation for feedback or performance evaluation. If you can establish a positive, respectful relationship, where the other person trusts that you see her as basically capable or that you see her good qualities, then you can offer feedback and suggestions without being met with defensiveness.

There is a large body of research from both education and business that supports the notion that students or employees perform better when the teacher or leader sees and acknowledges their capabilities; whereas these same people perform less well when the person in charge does not recognize their capabilities.

Think about your own experiences as an employee or student. Can you remember back to your school days? Was there perhaps a teacher who recognized your capabilities and communicated this to you? How did you perform in this teacher's class as compared with that of another teacher who was less encouraging? (You might ask a similar question with regard to your various supervisors at work.)

I remember my eighth-grade English teacher Miss Elder, who told me after reading one of my short stories that I had a flair for writing. These words stuck in my mind and made me want to achieve more, because I associated achievement with feeling good, with pleasure, with success. What if she had told me that my writing was sometimes stiff and colorless? While this may be an accurate criticism, maybe I needed to hear and believe the good news first. Maybe I needed to feel a bond of trust with this teacher before I would be prepared to deal well with any critical feedback. Her positive belief in me established a sense of common ground. With that as a starting point, she could then move in other directions with her comments, and I would be receptive.

Respectful communication builds trust and drives out fear. As we have seen, fear is what closes us off to learning. When we feel fear, we automatically revert to communication patterns designed to protect ourselves from loss or pain. The only trouble is, our protections also close us off from further learning. If we are not open to learning, it is unlikely that we will ever develop more resourceful strategies and, therefore, more self-trust. Our fears keep coming true—because we can't try anything new.

The way out of this vicious cycle is first to admit you are in it, and then to see what may be preventing you from opening yourself to learning from others. This will reveal what you need to let go of in order to get back to the Learning/Discovery attitude.

How Communicating to Build Trust Can Make You Indispensable to Your Organization and Customers

1. If you wish to take leadership or have any meaningful influence in today's learning organization, you must communicate in ways that make others feel safe to learn around you. Learning something new (especially if it is about oneself) often makes people feel quite vulnerable. They need to trust that you won't do them any harm, and this includes harm to their self-esteem or their ego.

When you behave respectfully, people trust that you will not judge or criticize their efforts. This helps them to be open to learning things that can enhance their effectiveness. When you have the ability to stimulate learning in others, you are contributing to the overall knowledge in your organization.

2. In today's contentious and litigious climate, trust is a delicate but critical ingredient for organizational effectiveness. To prevent expensive grievance procedures and litigation, people must feel free to approach you about problems before trust is lost. If you are approachable, you will be in an excellent position to take corrective measures when conflicts begin to brew. If you are not, you could find yourself in the middle of a problem about which you had no forewarning.

3. When your behavior is respectful, you will find that all of your relationships go more smoothly. You will spend less time on people problems stemming from other peoples' unresolved emotional issues, because you do not engage in the type of behavior that triggers these peoples' buttons. "Difficult people" is a two-way proposition. When your behavior helps people feel trusting and relaxed around you, they become less difficult.

4. When you become adept at interviewing and active listening, you have the essential tools needed for managing differences, resolving conflicts, and creating win-win solutions. In today's culturally diverse organization, you will encounter opportunities to use

these tools on a daily basis. Having tools like these in your reper-
toire makes you an invaluable resource.

How Communicating to Build Trust Can Help You Prevent or Respond to Crisis

1. Work gets done mainly in partnership with others. We need
to be able to quickly establish trusting partnerships if we are to
solve problems before they become crises.

2. When dealing with an unexpected surprise, we need to be
able to act quickly and get accurate information from others. The
more quickly we can build rapport and trust, the more quickly we
can respond to present or potential crises.

3. As the old forms and structures break down, you need to
engage with others in honest communication, free of hidden
agendas. Whether you are attempting to "sell" your resources for a
fee or chart a new cultural course, you can't do anything without
reliable input from all stakeholders.

4. When you are open to learning from others, you continually
increase your capacity to deal with diversity and complexity. Thus,
you continually expand your ability to deal with potential crises.

5. If a world crisis should occur, everyone will need a strong
network of relationships that they can depend on. Respectful, trustworthy communication builds such networks.

And Remember...

- The presence or absence of trust determines the validity of the
communications you receive.
- The intent to control shuts off the flow of communication. The
intent to learn opens it up.
- Seeking input and feedback from others shows you are open to
learning. It shows respect and builds trust.
- When you trust yourself to be able to handle the truth (rather
than "what you want to hear"), you can let go of the need to
control others.

CHAPTER EIGHT

Cultivate Both/And Thinking

To make sound business decisions, you need the ability to both hold your own position on an issue and at the same time consider alternative views. Both/And thinking gives you a way of holding several perspectives in your mind at once so you can consider them in relation to one another.

In dealing with differences, you have basically three choices: you can try to get other people to see things your way, you can accommodate so as to minimize conflict, or you can cultivate Both/And thinking. Many people assume they have only the first two choices—to dominate or to submit. But in the new workplace, with its tremendous complexity and diversity, these first two options lead to solutions that are often simplistic or shortsighted. Both/And thinking, as contrasted to Either/Or thinking, allows you to draw a bigger circle around two or more competing options so that you can see how they are complementary parts of a whole, instead of mutually exclusive. When you do this, you often find that there is a bit of truth on both sides—that reality is not *either* this *or* that, but more often *both* this *and* that.

There are many applications of Both/And thinking. We need to cultivate the capacity to consider divergent views and apparent contradictions alongside one another. We must be able to *both* assert our own views *and* respect the views of those who disagree with us. We need *both* the confidence to express our expertise *and* the humility to learn from people who are knowledgeable in areas we may not be. We need to *both* affirm and use our strengths *and* be mindful of our blind spots or limitations.

People who cannot tolerate disagreement, who cannot step outside the conflict long enough to consider all views, are not going to survive in the new workplace. Here is how Jerry and Phil, two business partners in a small computer software company, lost their business because of their inability to use Both/And thinking.

Jerry was known for his hot temper and forceful style. Phil was the more accommodating member of the partnership—easy going and eager to please. One day, Jerry came into the office very excited about an investment opportunity that promised to double the company's net worth over the next year. Phil had serious reservations about the advisability of moving company funds out of the more secure investments they presently held, but withheld his objections for fear of creating an uproar. When he tried to differ with Jerry in the past, he had found himself bombarded with angry accusations and insults. Phil agreed to let Jerry put 90 percent of the company's assets into the investment.

Two months later, the investment went sour, and Phil and Jerry lost their business. Both were operating from an Either/Or mindset—the idea that if one wins the other loses; or that if my partner disagrees with me, we cannot work together, so someone has to give in immediately. Phil knows now that if he and Jerry had been able to hit the conversation ball back and forth over the net a few times, exchanging ideas about alternatives, they could have developed a viable plan.

The new workplace contains enormous diversity in personal styles, values, language, and cultural expectations. And this diversity is rapidly increasing. If there ever was an era for learning to resolve conflicts and harmonize divergent interests, this is it.

I was working with a company recently where five people from the R&D department were trying to reach consensus about staffing and resource allocation. Attending were a twenty-five-year-old male Indian who wore a white turban, a forty-three-year-old African-American woman from Alabama, a fifty-five-year-old retired Army colonel who presented himself as a recovering alcoholic, a seventy-year-old Korean male, and a twenty-two-year-old woman who had recently emigrated from Eastern Europe.

All five of these people were well-educated scientists. And all were committed to team and company goals. This was their common ground. They were also individuals with quite different values about how money should be spent and who should be in charge. The tension in the room was palpable. I could sense the mounting frustration and the valiant efforts at self-control. They listened politely to one another, but it was obvious they were not really paying attention. Each was waiting for a chance to speak—for what that was worth, since no one was listening anyway!

How does work get done in such an environment? As we saw in the previous chapter, without an atmosphere of mutual respect, our communications are not trustworthy, and the system's capacity to learn from its own experience is impaired. Yet competitive, Either/Or environments are the rule rather than the exception in many organizations. Most of us were taught to think in Either/Or terms, to divide our world into mutually exclusive categories: this idea is good, that one is bad; she is motivated, he is unmotivated; I'm right, you're wrong; this product is marketable, that one is not.

In childhood, we had the grown-up view, which was superior, and the childish view, which was inferior. In adolescence, we had the in-group, which meant you were desirable, and the out-group, which meant you weren't good enough. In adulthood, we are either successes or failures. It is difficult to conceive that a person could be both right and wrong, both motivated and unmotivated, both successful in some areas and unsuccessful in others. When we pause to think more deeply about how things are, the Both/And view makes a lot of sense. Unfortunately, our thinking is often more automatic than accurate.

Anyone who would lead, facilitate, or attempt to improve any human system (including oneself) must understand that no person and no thing is all one way. No one is always right or always wrong. No one person or group can have all the answers. The good news about this is that we need each other's knowledge and input to help us see the whole picture or put together the puzzle. The bad news is we sometimes hate to admit it. Many of us just naturally feel that our way is the right way. The untrained mind has a tendency to go toward certainty, security, and arrogance. This is much easier than embracing uncertainty, the need for others' help, and the feeling of not being in control. We think we need certainty and control for our sense of well-being.

Dealing with different styles and opposing views on a daily basis can feel threatening. But it is only threatening if our security is based on having the right, or the most popular, answer.

In the new learning-oriented organization, we cannot afford such myopia. We will learn to value differing perspectives because these add breadth to our understanding and new possibilities to our problem-solving. We need to focus our sense of well-being and security on our ability to discover and create solutions using a variety of inputs, not on getting everybody to agree with us.

With Both/And thinking, people do not have to be similar in styles, or even in values, in order to work well together. There does need to be respect for each person's view and contribution. But we don't all have to think alike. Most of us have not learned how to feel at home in a room full of people who are clearly different from ourselves in some obvious way. Have you ever had the experience of being the only man or the only woman in a room full of people? Or the only person of your particular skin color or ethnicity? Or the only one not wearing a tie or a skirt? It is uncomfortable to be in the minority. We have learned to feel safer with people like ourselves. Both/And thinking helps us feel safe and powerful wherever we go because our intent is to learn from our differences, not to be like everyone else. We can learn so much from people who are different from ourselves when we make this our intention.

The ability to maintain your own position on an issue while at the same time entertaining other perspectives ensures that you won't ignore some potentially important piece of information just because it is uncomfortable to deal with. Again, as in previous chapters, we see that the ability to tolerate discomfort is essential if we wish to expand our capacity to deal with current reality. Chaos and conflict are uncomfortable, but by learning to embrace the increasing complexity of our world, we become more confident.

When you subscribe to the Either/Or mind-set, differences in style, interests, or viewpoint create fear and mistrust—as they did with Jerry and Phil. People either avoid conflict, or they attempt to control the other person. This drains an organization's resources.

The way out of this automatic habit is to step back and get a wider-angle view on the situation so you can see the relationships between things that formerly appeared separate or in opposition. Often when we do this, we find areas of common interest that we didn't see before. This promotes cooperation as both sides use their power and resources to help each other achieve their common goal instead of competing against each other.

My business partner and I once ended a very promising partnership prematurely because we got ourselves into an Either/Or, who's-to-blame, mind-set. As a result, we lost our ability to think objectively about our problem. We were in a situation where the monthly debt service on the loans we had taken out to start the business was so high that I was having to work a seventy-hour week. He was unable to bring in his share of new business, so it was all on my shoulders. All I could see was that he needed to work harder so he could generate more business. All he could see was that I was being critical and unfeeling. Because we took an adversarial posture with each other, we did not take the time or the care to consider all our options. We wanted the pain and conflict of our impasse to be over with as quickly as possible, so we short-circuited our decision-making process, jumping to the premature conclusion that we would have to end our partnership.

A few months after dissolving the business, we sat down together and did a postmortem on the decision. In that calmer, more thoughtful frame of mind, we looked at each other and realized: "We should have rented a less expensive building as our base of operations. That could have cut our monthly expenses by as much as seven thousand dollars. We didn't need such a large building." We felt sad and stupid that we had not even seen that as an option —because we were each so caught up in defending our positions and avoiding the discomfort of conflict.

Today's complex problems require a Both/And approach. When we fail to see a situation in its totality, we often solve one problem while creating another. Dissolving my business partnership is a case in point. Affirmative-action hiring is another.

Since the 1970s, government agencies and institutions who receive government funding have been required to show proof that they are places of equal-opportunity employment. Women and minorities have been afforded advantages in hiring that they have not had heretofore. This is an important problem, and it deserves attention.

Unfortunately, as this problem is being solved, another is being created. This is the problem of how to prevent resentment and backlash from those who have been denied employment because they are white and male. We need to recognize that every problem has more facets than any one interest group can perceive. That is why we need to consider the problem from the vantage point of both whites and people of color, both males and females, both management and labor. In the new workplace, we must learn to deal with problems in their full complexity.

Both/And thinking seeks to bring together all perspectives on a problem so that a well-informed and mutually agreeable course of action can be reached. This reduces the likelihood of creating unforeseen problems such as backlash or passive resistance from people and groups who have not bought into the solution.

Both/And thinking respects that different people have different life experiences, enabling them to more easily perceive particular aspects of reality and causing them to overlook other important aspects. No one can perceive everything. You may have especially sharp eyesight but impaired hearing, for example. In that case, you would need someone with better ears to fill you in on what you may be missing. That sort of difference, a difference in perceptual acuity, is an easy one to accept. A similar principle is operating if one person sees the costs of a proposed plan and the other sees the benefits. We need each other to see the whole picture. But, too often, such differences in viewpoint lead to a power struggle, instead of expanded perception. If our aim is personal learning for enhanced organizational effectiveness, then the person who sees things differently may have much to teach us. Jerry and Phil (at the beginning of this chapter) could have used their differences to keep their little company in balance. Unfortunately, their differences created more misunderstanding than perspective.

Turning Misunderstanding into Learning

Men and women typically get into misunderstandings because of their different communication styles. Rick and Janelle, while planning their department's upcoming quarterly retreat, have the following conversation: Rick says, "I think we should have it in New Orleans. It's nice there at that time of year." Janelle pauses, then says, "Okay." As we look in on the pair a month later, they are meeting to evaluate the event. Janelle discloses, "I never did think New Orleans was a good idea. I wanted to do it in Palm Beach." "What?" exclaims Rick in surprise. "I thought you agreed that it was nice there at this time of year."

As they attempt to unravel this misunderstanding, Janelle learns that Rick proposed New Orleans and then waited for her to object if she didn't agree. That's what he would have done: "Why didn't you speak up if you had a different idea?"

Rick learns that Janelle expected him to ask for her input if he wanted it. "I thought it was a done deal, since you didn't ask for my views. I always *invite* the other person to tell me what they think," she explained.

As Rick and Janelle continued to talk, they realized that their working relationship has been uncomfortable for quite some time. Janelle often felt "steamrolled" by Rick. Rick frequently felt judged by Janelle's silence. This awareness led to a conversation where each tried to get the other to change. "Just assert yourself," chided Rick. "Why don't you ask people for their input so they'll feel you're interested?" advised Janelle.

If we, as observers of this debate, can step back and see these two viewpoints from a Both/And perspective, we see the validity in both views: It is true, Janelle would do well to develop more assertiveness. It is also true that Rick could profitably learn something from her knack for drawing people out in conversations. If the pair could look at their differences this way, both could come away with important personal learnings.

Both/And thinking includes the following ideas:

- Each of us holds only a partial view of any situation, and we need others' inputs to see the rest of the picture. Both/And thinking makes organizational learning possible because it promotes the type of communication that can fill in the gaps in each worker's knowledge.
- Everything and every quality that exists has more than one side to it—an obvious outward manifestation and a subtle, hidden

aspect. People, for example, have both their positive, well-developed attributes and their sometimes hidden or less-developed aspects. We need one another as mirrors, to reflect to us our underdeveloped sides, and to show us how to round them out.

- Because of the at-least-two-sidedness of everyone, we are all ambivalent to a degree. You may both want to succeed at your job and at the same time feel cautious about the added responsibility that comes with success. You may both wish to learn a new skill and fear what you will have to go through during the learning process—like feeling awkward at first. It is best not to overidentify with either side, but instead to realize that you are *both* eager to learn *and* afraid.

- Because of our discomfort with our inner ambivalence, we often project our inner conflicts outward onto our interpersonal relationships. The outer power struggles with others often mirror the inner struggles we are having with ourselves. Thus, if I am in conflict over how to balance work and relaxation in my life, I may find myself in a relationship power struggle where one of us overworks and the other overplays. This may explain why opposites so often attract (and later repel) in both love and work relationships. Jerry and Phil's relationship was an example of this principle. Each represented the other's hidden, or "shadow," side. Jerry had learned out of fear to keep his "accommodating side" hidden so that no one would ever take advantage of him. Phil had learned to keep his dominance hidden, so everyone would like him. Each was struggling within himself to find a better balance between accommodating and dominating. The outer struggle between them mirrored each man's inner disharmony.

- Both/And thinking offers a very practical approach for dealing with the people we find most difficult. If I am bugged by my coworker's self-centeredness, for example, this may reflect an unconscious struggle within myself regarding this unappealing trait. Perhaps I have trouble admitting to myself any feeling that looks even remotely self-centered—so as a result, I tend to let self-centered people walk all over me. This is why I find these people so difficult. But they can be teachers for me as well, because in their presence I am pushed to behave more assertively in order to keep myself from being overpowered. Phil could have used Jerry as his teacher in this way, and he eventually did.

- It is possible to operate both on behalf of the whole (group, company, marriage, etc.) and on behalf of yourself at the same time. You can train yourself to see both the parts and the whole at once. A good group facilitator or third-party mediator does this. So does any good leader or executive. A leader doesn't feel good about what she has done until everyone on the team feels good. A leader has the capacity to hold in mind "the good of the whole" and behave accordingly.
- It is possible to serve values or ends that might appear to be mutually exclusive or contradictory. You can be both demanding of excellence and compassionate in your treatment of people, for example. You can listen openly to a viewpoint that you vehemently disagree with and at the same time retain your commitment to your own views or values. This is essential for being a good negotiator, a good group facilitator, a good team player, or a good parent.
- Paradox is a fact of life. The harder you try to control the outcome of your efforts, the less in control you feel. The more you try to overcome or escape from some feared outcome, the more this feared thing pursues and haunts you.

Both/And thinking draws a bigger circle around things that might ordinarily seem contradictory or unrelated. It reveals the subtler relationships and interdependencies between things. It enables us to see the pattern within the chaos, the emerging truth in the confusion, and the meaning in the pain. It helps us reconcile the irreconcilable.

Here are three situations as viewed through the Either/Or-versus-the-Both/And lens:

Either/Or	Both/And
That employee is unmotivated. We should fire her.	Most employees feel both the wish to excel and the wish to goof off. What working conditions will foster this person's wish to excel?
Management isn't concerned	It is possible to attend both to

about employees' needs. It only cares about profits.	individual needs and to company needs. Most companies try to do both, but they may need help from the employees in learning how to best serve individual needs. Creating organizations that support employees is the job of both management and other employees.
If our company grows any bigger, our responsiveness to customer and employee needs will suffer.	Let's search for ways of structuring ourselves that retain the small-company responsiveness alongside the efficiency advantages of a larger firm.

To help you develop your Both/And skills, here are six things you can begin to do right away:

1. Embrace paradox.
2. Exercise your "thinking muscles" in new ways.
3. Use Both/And approaches in team-building.
4. Use your everyday conflicts as opportunities to let go of control.
5. Identify the polarities in your personality and in your relationships.
6. Balance the polarities in your personality.

The first two of the above-mentioned items helps you let go of ordinary thinking habits so you can look at problems from more than one angle. The last four ways apply Both/And thinking to managing differences. The goal of all six is to build your capacity to learn, create, and solve problems in an increasingly complex environment.

1. Embrace Paradox

Albert Einstein helped scientists see that "you cannot solve a problem using the same mode of thinking that gave rise to the problem," or "you can't solve the problem at the level of the problem." Both/And thinking gets us above the level of the problem so we can see the relationships between things formerly thought to be separate or mutually exclusive. It gives us a wider, broader perspective. It puts into one container things that might at first seem contradictory.

Any time you see the complementarity or connection between things that might ordinarily be seen as separate or opposing, you are engaging in Both/And thinking. Most of us have had the experience of both caring about a person and being frustrated with him at one and the same time. This is a Both/And moment. And you have probably been in a situation where you felt both very eager to try something new and at the same time afraid. Life is full of Both/And moments. The essence of the experience is recognizing the underlying unity of opposing forces. When you expand your viewpoint this way, solutions become apparent that you never would have imagined.

The Paradox of Control

If you can become fascinated with the paradoxes in your life, you will not be frustrated by them.

Have you ever had any of these fascinating experiences?

- The harder you tried to create a particular impression on someone, the less successful you were; but when you relaxed and let yourself be ordinary, you made a very positive impression.
- The more you tried to get someone to behave the way you wanted her to, the more she resisted; but when you let her do things her own way, she seemed more interested in learning about your wishes.
- The more you tried to get employees to use your logical, organized methods, the more chaotic things became; but when you trusted each person's unique work style, the work got done in a more orderly fashion.

Why do things often happen this way? Are people out to thwart you or teach you a lesson? Or is there another principle at work here? I believe the principle at work in these three instances is what I call "the paradox of control." When you are attached to having something happen in a certain way, that is usually when you will be frustrated. When you let go of your need to control and relax about the outcome, you are more apt to be satisfied. Here's why:

Attachment to having what you want is almost always accompanied by a fear that you won't get it. This fear tends to inhibit the free exchange of energy between you and your surroundings. There is tension in the air. You are less open, less able to respond creatively to what is happening. You are cut off from your connectedness with others. When you are afraid, your control needs increase. People can feel your attempts to control the situation. Things tend to become discordant because your coworkers and friends feel tense, self-protective and disconnected around you.

I have a friend, Anabel, whose situation clearly illustrates the paradox of control. Anabel frequently laments to me, "I want so much for my employees to like and respect me, but they always take me for granted—no matter how much I do for them. They seem to feel uncomfortable when I praise them or ask if I can help them."

As I think about my friend now, recalling the stories she has told me about the people at work, I know why they don't appear to like her. Whenever she is in their presence, she is trying so hard to make a good impression that the people around her feel her efforts to control their responses. This leads them to erect protective defenses so as not to be controlled by her intense need to be liked.

Can you think of a situation where the response or outcome you got was the exact opposite of the one you wanted? Is it possible that you wanted a particular outcome so much that you interfered with its happening? And that if you had not inter-*feared,* if you had let nature take its course, things might have come out quite differently?

The Paradox of Avoidance

Related to the paradox of control is another familiar one: the more you try to avoid a situation, the more it seems to recur in your life. Its reappearance may be in different disguises, but you know that same sinking feeling every time it happens.

There's an old saying, "You can run, but you can't hide." This saying summarizes the principle behind the paradox of avoidance.

If there is a feature in your character that repeatedly causes you pain or frustration, this feature will haunt you until the day you die unless you face it squarely and deal with it.

No matter where Dederick worked, he always avoided dealing face-to-face with anyone in authority. If he had a question about how a procedure was done, he would ask a peer, never a manager. If he was supposed to present a service or information to anyone higher up, he would attempt to delegate this task, or he would get sick so someone else would have to step in for him. What was he avoiding? In private conversations with me, he disclosed that he didn't want to risk being criticized. He could take it from peers, but not from someone who had power over him. You can guess what the result was of his avoidance-of-criticism pattern. He was the subject of much criticism by management for just this pattern— but not to his face.

Have you ever tried to make sure *that* doesn't happen? Or to make sure *that never happens to me again?* And did it happen again? Often, if it's something you put a lot of energy into avoiding, it will happen again, and maybe even again and again. This is because the thing you seek to avoid is related to something you have not yet come to terms with in yourself. Jerry tried at all costs to avoid being pushed around, because he had not come to terms with the part of him that was afraid of being overly accommodating and controlled. He needed to embrace this other side of himself, the accommodating side, as well as the aggressive side. When you embrace both sides of a push-pull within yourself, when you embrace your wholeness, then you stop running away from yourself.

The Paradox of Change

To get where you want to be, you must start where you are. The most effective way to change anything about yourself is to begin by acknowledging and accepting your present situation. As we saw in Chapter Four, compassionately accepting and taking responsibility for your present situation is the first and most important step in creating change. When you try to overcome a problem (such as fear of criticism) by pretending it doesn't exist, you are not taking responsibility for the problem—so you are not empowered to do anything about it.

Many people feel that "accepting themselves" means giving too much latitude to the negative qualities they wish to get rid of. The truth is that if you try to get rid of something by denying it, this alienates it from the rest of the self so it cannot be reached or influenced. An alienated or disowned part of the personality recedes into the subconscious mind. From there, it may express itself in ways you are not aware of and therefore cannot influence.

Fiona had a deep mistrust of men, but she could not admit it. On the surface, she appeared to be quite supportive of the men who worked in her area. She even used her manner of dress and makeup, which were quite seductive, to try and mask her unconscious wish to push men away. She didn't realize it, but the men who worked with her reported that they always felt tense and on guard around her.

One day, when she was standing alone near the copy machine, a male coworker, Edward, decided to break the ice with a little humor. He made a flirtatious remark that she found offensive. This triggered a fear reaction in Fiona that caused her to blow up in anger at Edward and complain to his supervisor that he was sexually harassing her.

This unfortunate incident led to several conversations between Fiona and her manager about the feelings that had been stimulated by Edward's remark. She was able to confront some fears about men that she had been carrying since her teen years. Once she became aware of these fears, she could take responsibility for them. She used this crisis as an opportunity to learn about the roots of her fears and to do what she could to uproot them. If she had not been forced to acknowledge her fears, she would never have learned to let them go.

The Paradox of Excellence

Many people report overworking themselves almost to the breaking point in an effort to achieve their very best. We have all heard stories of how unmercifully some people push themselves in order to feel good enough. The paradoxical result is, the more they push, the less adequate they feel—and often, the less effective they are as well. When they let go of this excessive drive to excel, they progress faster.

When Ronald found himself getting seriously overweight, he decided that life was too short to overwork himself the way he had been doing. He put himself on a new routine, which included free time for either golf or a long walk every other day. At first, he worried that this would take too much productive time out of his day. After two months of this routine, his manager called him in for a conference to find out why his sales had nearly doubled in the past month. Ronald didn't know if he should tell his manager that golfing and walking played a big part in his success.

Once again, we see how unexpected success can come from letting go instead of pushing. Perhaps this is because when you do not trust yourself, your relationship with yourself is an either/or, adversarial one. This creates inner tension. You don't feel good about yourself, so you are not as effective.

Paradoxes like these reveal the complex, messy, multilayered, both-and-ness of life. The real reasons things happen are often not clear. Things do not come out as expected, but often the exact opposite. Causality is not altogether conscious and linear. The contents of your subconscious mind have a big impact on the results you get. There are many causes for any one outcome.

When making important decisions in a world of rapid knowledge creation, you need to look at things from as many angles as possible.

2. Exercise New ''Thinking Muscles''

I was once a consultant to a paper manufacturer in Maine, a company that was split into two factions. One group felt that the company should develop technology to recycle its effluent waste rather than dumping it raw into the nearby river. The other group, which included the vice president for finance, felt that this would be too costly. The first group argued that the surrounding communities were angry at the company, and that this would eventually backfire. The other group protested, "We'll cross that bridge when we come to it." Here we see one group being more concerned with the economics of the situation and the other being more concerned about ecology and community relations.

The situation reached a crisis at the annual off-site planning meeting, which I facilitated. Tension between the two camps was evident. People were noticeably curt with those in the opposing group, even during meals and breaks. Rather than trying to resolve the polarization by debate, I invited both groups to join with me in an exploration of the advantages and disadvantages, the pros and cons, of the idea of developing the new recycling technology. The entire group looked first at all the pluses of the idea, with everyone contributing to the brainstorming process. Then we gave equal time to considering all the minuses of the idea for the new technology. This *pro-and-then-con technique* gave the whole group the experience of being on the same side—first on one side of the argument and then on the other. The technique is useful for both group conflicts and conflicts within oneself. It gets the two sides out of struggle and blame and into productive discussion.

The more blaming that occurs by one part of the system toward another part, the more difficult it will be for the various parts of the system to agree on the need for change. If we are to foster an honest appraisal of the present situation, it is very important to refrain from judgment or blame. These emotions create unnecessary resistance in one part of the system to the information offered by another part. Other people will resist what you have to say if they feel blamed. We saw in Chapter Seven how important respectful communication is for mutual problem-solving.

If you are experiencing an inner struggle between two parts of yourself, the same principle applies. If you blame yourself for being where you are, this will create internal resistance; and your conflicting "sides" will not be able to hear one another. Each side has information vital to the solution of the problem. If you believe this, then it is important to find a way to get the two (or more) sides to listen respectfully to what the other has to say.

Meta-Skill Builder 32:
The Toothpick Brain Teaser

In workshops dealing with creativity and change, I often give groups the following activity, which you can try with your team. I hold up a toothpick (or other familiar object), saying: "This is an ordinary toothpick. But a toothpick can have many uses other than picking your teeth. It could be used to open a tube of glue. It could be a splint for a praying mantis with a broken leg. And I'm sure you can think of many more alternative uses for this one object." Then each person finds a partner, and I give each pair a toothpick. Their task is to brainstorm and write down as many different uses for this toothpick as they can dream up. People are amazed at how many creative alternatives they come up with. This is a good exercise to play on a car trip with friends or family. People of all ages can enjoy it. You can do it in pairs or individually. Let each group member have a turn at selecting the object to be considered.

Meta-Skill Builder 33:
Taking Alternative Viewpoints

Here is another exercise to get you looking at one event from several different perspectives. Imagine you are watching a couple speeding down the freeway in their BMW. The man is driving, and his wife is in the passenger seat. A motorcycle patrolman appears behind them as if out of nowhere, his lights flashing. Now imagine what each of the three might be thinking or feeling right now. Be the husband, and put yourself in his place. Then be the wife. What is she thinking? Finally, see yourself on that motorcycle chasing this pair. This exercise builds your ability to shift your perspective at will. It's fun and often illuminating—especially if you compare your ideas about the scene with those of someone you know well.

You can do this type of exercise any time you watch a movie or television show. Notice that you will initially identify most easily with one of the characters in the scene. Then consciously place yourself in the other roles.

Meta-Skill Builder 34:
The Pro-and-Then-Con Technique

Think of an everyday conflict in which you have been at odds with another person. Maybe it is something as simple as choosing the best route to the grocery store, the longer route with less traffic or the shorter, more congested route. The next time you meet with this person, instead of each of you taking your own position and arguing for it, try the pro-and-then-con technique. Both of you together think of all the pros and all the cons for the longer route. Then both consider all pros and cons for the shorter route. This stretches your mind and creates a climate for mutual problem-solving. It can also be a lot of fun.

3. Use Both/And Approaches in Team-Building

It is important that all members of a work team appreciate each other's natural strengths and accept each other's limitations. Both/And thinking gives people permission to admit both their strengths and their limitations. It validates talking about both what we do well and what we are still learning how to do. When we are candid about disclosing our limitations or "growing edges," then the team can design mechanisms to compensate for these. If a member of the team is likely to take on too much work and then renege on commitments, for example, while she is learning to manage this problem, the rest of the team can help her (and themselves) by checking in regularly to see if she needs to renegotiate any of the agreements she has made.

In the leadership team of a large metropolitan hospital, the three top administrators, Sheryl, Maureen, and Frank, had three very different patterns of strengths and growing edges. Sheryl's style was very authoritative. She had a way of inspiring confidence in colleagues and members of the community. That was the good news. The bad news was that she had so much confidence in her own way of doing things that she found herself getting impatient with others. The people working for her often felt either criticized or superfluous. Learning to empower others was a growing edge for her.

Maureen's style was more inclusive and collegial. She had a natural, easy way of asking others for their inputs and of allowing them to take the time they needed to get assignments clarified. The bad news for Maureen was that she lacked confidence in her own judgment. Her growing edge was to develop more trust in her own opinions and to risk putting these on the table in team meetings.

Frank was the visionary on the team. He inspired the other two with the big pictures he could paint. On the down side, he was not at all comfortable with people. Most of his attention went toward possibilities for improvement and expansion, not toward the day-to-day operations of the hospital. His growing edge was to learn how to deal realistically with the way things are—to be more forgiving toward his employees and more accepting of the frustrations of being a manager.

You probably know, from being in situations with people like Frank or Maureen or Sheryl, that people with different styles often push each other's buttons. But these same differences that push buttons can be used to *make yourself*—to develop the growing edges that are revealed by the fact that you have these buttons.

In doing team-building, I like to guide group members to identify the buttons that tend to get triggered in each relationship. The idea here is that we will (1) each take responsibility for the fact that we do have our buttons or areas of hypersensitivity, and (2) try not to push the other's buttons.

When team members have been through a process in which they disclose buttons and growing edges along with being acknowledged for their strengths, people are more accepting of each other, and buttons don't get pushed as often. Teammates will discuss ways to assist each other in achieving their personal and professional growth goals instead of getting irritated with each other.

4. Use Everyday Conflicts as Opportunities for Learning

Kurt and Marshall were partners in a small real estate development firm. Kurt complained that he couldn't get his partner Marshall to take action on any of the proposals that he made. Marshall complained that Kurt's investment proposals were not well researched. Kurt insisted that this was Marshall's job, not his. "After all, you're the numbers man—I'm just the contractor." And so it went, each one protesting, "I can't do my job until you do yours."

When Kurt and Marshall first decided to go into partnership two years earlier, they assumed that their differences would be an asset, that Kurt's talent for finding potential properties would be nicely balanced by Marshall's ability to cautiously evaluate them. But after working together for less than a year, their differences had become intolerable. Marshall was accusing Kurt of "wanting to make an offer on anything with a price tag," while Kurt complained that Marshall was "unwilling to even sign a check for the phone bill without researching every item on it."

They were stuck in a "Looker versus Leaper" power struggle (from the phrase "look before you leap"). Kurt was the risk-taking Leaper, while Marshall was the more cautious Looker. They began exploring their differences by reviewing the history of their working relationship. Doing this reminded them of the feelings they used to have about their differences, of how they originally decided to work together because of their belief that in any real estate deal, *both* caution *and* risk are needed. They traced the history of their partnership from this initial Both/And attraction to its current polarized state.

In looking at why they were initially drawn to the idea of working together, they got into a discussion about what life had taught each of them. They did this by sharing stories from their childhood. Marshall's had been characterized by upheaval, unpredictability and insecurity. Kurt's had been calm, predictable, and boring. By now, it was becoming obvious to them why they approached the unknown so differently.

Their stories support the idea that people get into power struggles because *what one person has underlearned,* in the course of his lifetime, *the other has overlearned.* Kurt had underlearned caution, which Marshall had overlearned. Marshall had underlearned risk-taking, which Kurt had overlearned. The polarization reveals what each person needs to learn. And if a dialogue can be created, there may be the opportunity in this relationship to finally learn one's underlearned trait.

As Kurt and Marshall continued to explore their differences with genuine interest, each man saw where he himself was a bit off balance. Each came to value some of what the other could teach him. And they stopped blaming one another for the stagnation of the business. They correctly diagnosed their problem as each one's inability to trust his own "other side," not the partner. Your other side is the side of yourself you have repressed or denied. You don't know it very well, so it's hard to trust it.

With all this open communication, you might expect their business problem to be solved in a way that drew them into closer partnership, but in this case, it was not. Insights and feelings do not always translate into immediate behavior change. Marshall, while he truly valued becoming more of a risk-taker, could not take the leap fast enough to save the partnership. He still did not have sufficient trust in his own capacity to tolerate risk. Kurt, because he was learning to recognize his own fears, felt a profound respect for Marshall's pace, but he could not completely overcome his impatience to risk more. So, instead of remaining in partnership, the two dissolved the formal partnership and decided to use one another as business advisers.

At present, when I check in on these two men and their separate businesses, they both seem happier now that they are apart. But they affirm that the friendship has been strengthened and that they really have become teachers for one another.

Both/And conflict resolution helps a system become conscious of and integrate its hidden side. Each time this occurs, a higher, more expanded level of consciousness or view of reality is reached.

Most systems tend to polarize, or fall out of balance, at some point during their life cycle. We saw this with Kurt and Marshall's relationship. In my book *Beyond the Power Struggle,* I describe the dynamics of how the "power struggle stage" often follows an initial period of hope and harmony. This phenomenon is a reflection of the natural process of growth in human systems. If the system can become more aware of this tendency to become polarized in either/or opposition to one another, the people involved can look for the polarity (Both/And-ness) underlying the unfortunate polarization. In seeing their polarity, Kurt and Marshall realized that each had something the other really needed to learn in order to become more whole as a person. Today's organizations need people who can see the possibility of learning from the people who initially bug them or irritate them.

5. Identify the Polarities in Your Inner Life and Outer Life

According to the concept of polarities, everything has another side to it. If you are a *saver,* for example, there's a *spender* in there somewhere just waiting for an opportunity to get out (perhaps "when you get rich.") Or if you're a real laid back *dawdler* type, you may be using this to mask the *scurrier* within (that is, your tendency to push yourself). Over the course of a lifetime, a person's self-concept tends to become *polarized,* so we see ourselves as either happy or sad, either energetic or slow-moving. We need to develop the ability to sense our *polarity,* our Both/And-ness. The truth is you can be sometimes a saver and at other times a spender, sometimes calm and sometimes in a hurry, sometimes happy and at other times sad. You can even be both happy and sad at once, with one of these feelings being just a bit more foreground while the other is more in the background. This illustrates the idea of polarity as opposed to polarization: you're not either one or the other; you're sometimes one and sometimes the other, and often a combination of both.

If you can learn to deal with this sort of complexity within your own personality, it's a short step to dealing more effectively with the ever-increasing complexity of your outer world.

Meta-Skill Builder 35: Your Inner Dialogue

Here is an exercise to illuminate the polarities that are important in your inner life:

Take out about twenty three-by-five cards, and on each one, list the various parts of your personality. You might also add to this list the *roles* you play in life, such as mother, sister, friend, engineer etc. Then rank these parts according to which ones are most and least close to your essential self, or according to which ones you could most and least easily live without.

When your parts are represented on cards, place opposite each other any cards that represent inner conflict or antipathy.

Choose one internal polarity that feels significant or problematical, such as your "at-work self" versus your "real self" or your inner responsible parent versus your inner playful child.

In writing, create a dialogue between these two parts, just as if you were writing a play with these two characters in it. Here is an internal dialogue written by Bruce, a physicist for a high-tech research company. The dialogue is between his solitary self, whom he named "The Loner" and his social self, whom he named "Sonny."

SONNY: Why don't you want to go out to lunch with the other guys? They ask you all the time. I'm getting tired of just sitting in the lab and eating my salad by myself.

LONER: I like to get things done. It's a big waste of time going out and taking an hour or more just to eat. I'm satisfied just doing what I want to do.

SONNY: You never have any fun. And besides, a lot of important information gets talked about over lunch. You would have a chance to give your opinions about the proposed restructuring of the department. What are you afraid of?

LONER: I am not afraid.

SONNY: I think you are. Is it wasting time, or is it something else? Are you uncomfortable with conversation? Are you afraid you can't hold your own with those smarter guys?

LONER: I'm as smart as they are. You know that.

SONNY: I know that, but do you?

LONER: Well, I have doubts, but so what. That's not it.

SONNY: So what is it?

LONER: Okay, maybe I am uncomfortable around a bunch of people. So I have a right to stay here at lunch, don't I?

SONNY: Could I do anything to help you feel more comfortable around people?

LONER: Don't try to pressure me. I'll just withdraw and clam up.

SONNY: Let me ask one more thing, and then I'll back off. What would it take to just try going out to lunch one time to see how it goes? Couldn't we do an experiment?

LONER: Now you're talking my language. An experiment. So if it doesn't work, we don't have to do it again, right?

SONNY: Okay, and what do you mean "if it doesn't work"?

LONER: Oh, I guess if I can't stand it and feel like I have to get out of there.

SONNY: I'd like to help you so you don't get that feeling. If it gets too uncomfortable, let me know and we can take a break and go outside for a few minutes. How's that sound?

LONER: I'd be okay with going out to lunch with them once and seeing how it feels.

SONNY: If it feels bad, we could go outside or we could go to the men's room and have a dialogue like this one.

LONER: I don't know you well enough yet for that.

SONNY: Well, let's keep getting to know one another better. Okay?
LONER: Okay.

After Bruce wrote out this internal dialogue between his two sides, he reported that he felt friendlier toward other people. He said it was because he now felt a little friendlier toward himself. The dialogue could have gone on longer. There was not yet a clear agreement between his two parts. But even a few minutes of this self-talk process helped him feel more trusting of himself.

He also reported that he felt more "balanced." He said the internal tension that he usually felt had decreased somewhat, and he didn't feel he had to watch himself so closely.

It is interesting to note that Bruce reported feeling more relaxed around others. This is an example of how an inner struggle or polarization tends to play itself out in your outer life. And when you find more harmony internally, this, too, carries over into your relationships with others.

This inner-dialogue process can also be done with more than two parts. In this case, you would imagine the three or more parts seated around a conference table all giving their individual inputs on an issue. Again, it is not necessary for all the voices to achieve agreement.

Meta-Skill Builder 36:
Dialogue with a Difficult Person

Some people have difficulty carrying on an inner dialogue like Bruce did in the previous meta-skill builder. If such self-talk feels like a foreign language to you, here is another method for identifying the inner polarity that creates struggle in your relationships.

Think of a relationship that causes you discomfort, frustration, pain, anger, or the like. Now write the script for a conversation with this other person. It need not be a conversation you would actually have. The important thing is to play out both sides in your own mind. Here is Bruce's conversation with his boss, Thomas:

BRUCE: Why haven't you consulted me about the restructuring you're planning?

THOMAS: I didn't think you cared what we did. You seem content to just do your work and stay out of the administrative end.

BRUCE: Well, this is one thing I'm interested in. I'm offended that you didn't know that.

THOMAS: Well, thank you for coming forth. I hardly ever know what you're thinking. And I'd like to.

BRUCE: You don't ever show me that. You never come and ask me.

THOMAS: I know. You aren't easy to approach. You always seem so busy. I'm afraid to waste your time with trivia.

BRUCE: Okay. I see what's going on. I want you to come to me, and you expect me to let you know if I'm interested. You think I'm more confident and assertive than I really am.

This written dialogue was never played out in real life. It was purely for Bruce's personal learning. He reported that he learned something very important about himself and his relationships from doing it: other people tend to treat him the way he treats himself —they ignore his social needs much of the time. He concluded two things from this: first, if he wants others to pay attention to his social needs, he will have to learn how to pay better attention to these himself; and second, his projection onto others that they don't want his input is inaccurate. They are probably afraid to bother him. So if he wants others to feel free to bother him more, he will probably need to risk bothering them sometimes. We see once again how the polarities that create conflict in your outer life often mirror those within your own personality.

6. Balance Your Inner Polarities

When someone's behavior bugs you, this often means that they have something important to teach you. They have become quite good at something that you may not be much good at. Or they easily express some trait that you would judge harshly in yourself. Perhaps it is a generally unappealing trait, such as selfishness. But if someone's selfishness bugs you, it is a signal that there is something you need to learn about this quality. Maybe you are not "selfish" enough—or to use another term, perhaps you are not attentive enough to your own needs or feelings. Maybe you suppress your selfishness because you learned a long time ago that it was unacceptable.

In doing research for *Beyond the Power Struggle,* I found that relationships tend to become polarized when two people differ on some important behavioral dimension. If you are a saver, for example, and your partner is a spender, you may find yourself becoming tighter and tighter as the relationship progresses—becoming much more of a saver than you ordinarily would be. The other's style triggers a fear in you. You fear she will spend and spend, and all will be lost, unless you keep the lid on by saving more.

A situation that polarizes like this reveals that each party has something to learn from the other. She has something to learn about saving. You have something to learn about spending. Maybe you need to learn to trust yourself more in this area, or perhaps to take better care of yourself by allowing yourself more in this area, or perhaps to take better care of yourself by allowing yourself to spend a bit more. But since you have not yet learned this, your partner's behavior pushes your button. To get beyond the power struggle and out of your artificially polarized position, try on the idea that her spending would not but you so much if you could connect more with the spender within you.

Instead of trying to change the other person (Security/Control), learn from her (Learning/Discovery). There are two important aspects of this type of learning:

1. *Learning about yourself.* What experiences and early lessons have led you to become a saver who is perhaps unaware of or judgmental toward your "inner spender"? Is this an area of your life where you might benefit from being more balanced? What fears or beliefs do you hold that keep you stuck where you are?

2. *Learning from the other.* There is probably something this other person knows how to do that you could learn and benefit from. Observe this person in action—what would you wish to emulate, and what can you learn from her mistakes or excesses? Let your mind be curious and open instead of critical. This shift in your attitude will accomplish several things:

• You will identify whatever it is that you need to learn or are avoiding about your own capacity for spending;
• You will experience the tangible benefits of the Learning/Discov-

ery attitude—of putting a higher value on learning about yourself than on being right or being in control; and
• The two of you will get along better. When you are open to learning from the other, she will feel your respect and become more open to learning from you. If the two of you are in a relationship, it is also likely that she will begin to connect more with her "inner saver," which is probably something she needs to learn from you but can't when you two are in a power struggle.

In today's complex organization, everyone's voice needs to be heard. No one group member, not even the company president, can possess all the information necessary to guide the group's actions. In order to work well with people whose perspectives differ from yours, you must develop the ability to learn from people without necessarily sharing their point of view. When you draw a big circle around the various viewpoints, they can all be considered in relation to one another. When everyone on the team possesses this skill there is a calm, open attitude toward differences and an ability to learn and create together.

How Both/And Thinking Can Make You Indispensable to Your Organization and Customers

1. While international economic barriers are being removed in this global business climate, you need to be comfortable and competent in a very large arena. As various parts of the global network become more integrated, it becomes increasingly important to know how to learn from people whose worldview is quite different from your own. Both/And thinking allows you to cooperate and collaborate with people and groups whom you might have avoided previously, thus expanding the size of the world you can operate in.

2. As a Both/And thinker, you are better equipped to spot opportunities for collaborative, mutually beneficial alliances with customers, suppliers, investors, and the public.

3. Within your organization, you will be well poised to help your organization cut down on the waste caused by interdepart-

mental isolationism or competition. Because of your ability to see the big picture, you can see if different departments are duplicating each other's efforts—so you can take action to eliminate the waste and duplication that often occur when departments have competitive relationships or overlapping functions.

4. The successful organization of the future will be structured entirely differently than today's organization. To assist your organization with this fundamental redesign task, you will need to be able to consider a large number of elements in relationship to each other, honoring each part's contribution to the whole.

5. To make sound, sustainable decisions, you need the capacity to hold apparently contradictory views in mind long enough to discover the common ground that unites them. Both/And thinking gives you this capacity to think more clearly about complex problems.

How Both/And Thinking Can Help You Prevent or Respond to Crisis

1. In a crisis situation, it is quite likely that different people will advocate different approaches to the problem. Both/And thinking equips you to "build bridges instead of walls" and discover solutions that will be acceptable to all sides, thus achieving more lasting agreement.

2. In solving problems of crisis proportions, you will need to step out of your ordinary mind-set that tries to treat each element of the problem separately, without regard for their interdependence. You cannot afford to be shortsighted or simplistic. You need to view problems in their full context. Usually, the reason the crisis has occurred is because the people involved were not able to treat the problem in its entirety.

3. As the old forms break down, we all need to cooperate in discovering and creating new solutions. It becomes essential that people have the ability to converse and solve problems with others whose views they may not understand or agree with.

And Remember...

- The new workplace is full of paradox and apparent contradiction. When you try to sort things out into neat little boxes, putting success over here and failure over there, acceptance in this box and rejection in that one, you violate something about what I like to call *the natural messiness of life.*
- There are two sides to everything: a light and a dark side, a side we enjoy and a side we'd rather not deal with. This is the nature of life. One of life's challenges is learning to take "the bad with the good." The way to do this is through being open to learning what the dark side has to teach you.
- People do not have to share similar values or styles in order to work well together.
- Differences between yourself and others tend to become polarized when you have underlearned something (such as assertiveness) that the other has overlearned. To get beyond polarization, both parties need to recognize that they have something important to learn from the other.
- When you understand and accept the Both/And-ness within your own personality, it becomes easier to deal gracefully with differences and conflicts between people and groups.

Be a Team Learner

Just as we must come to terms with the continuous change process occurring within us as individuals, we must also understand and trust the process by which groups learn and develop.

In his ground-breaking book *The Fifth Discipline: The Art and Practice of the Learning Organization,* Peter Senge states, "Mastering *team learning* will be a critical step in building learning organizations." Team learning grows from confronting and solving problems together in ways that teach you more about your own and other team members' resources and growing edges. Personal learning is always a major component of team learning. If individuals are not actively interested in becoming more effective people, they will not help the group become a more effective team.

You know team learning is taking place when there is an increase in the group's capacity to:

• make use of each member's unique contribution;
• make decisions and take action as a unit; and
• anticipate the need for change without waiting for a crisis.

Sometimes, team learning begins with your recognition that you lack one or more of these capacities.

The six of us were sailing my company's forty-seven-foot sloop down the Sacramento River as part of a three-day team-building retreat. Besides me, the team's consultant, there was Charlie, CEO of a large auto-parts-manufacturing company; Andy, his VP for finance; Rick, the marketing VP; Ned, the manufacturing VP, and Hank, the engineering VP. Andy and I were the only experienced sailors among the group. Each of the others had been trained for a specific task on the boat.

The purpose of the retreat was to develop their ability to operate more as a cooperative unit and less as individuals competing for company resources. They had a history of secretiveness and divisiveness that was damaging to both morale and profits.

We had chosen the river instead of the nearby Pacific Ocean because ocean waters can be quite unpredictable, and we didn't want to get surprised with any major physical threats. We thought we would just set sail in the morning, have some time to get used to working together in a relaxed atmosphere, and then dock for a late lunch at one of the many restaurants along the river's edge. After that, the plan was to sail back home and spend the evening reflecting on what we had observed about ourselves as a team.

That was the plan.

It was not in our plan to run aground. But a mile before we were ready to dock for lunch in Rio Vista, with Ned at the helm and Hank reading the depth sounder, Charlie called our attention to the centerboard winch—which was at that moment being torn off the deck by pressure from below. First, we heard an ominous creaking sound, and then a loud crack, indicating that something below had snapped in two. We figured it was the centerboard. The centerboard is a retractable rudder that can be raised and lowered as needed. In this case, in such shallow waters, it should not have been in the lowered position. But someone had not been paying attention.

Andy and I got to work trying to raise the centerboard to prevent further damages, but there was already a large hole in the deck where the winch had once been secured. And even though we were able to free up what was left of the centerboard, we were not able to get the boat off the shoals.

We were stuck in the mud, and hungry to boot. The higher tide, which could set us free, was at least six hours off. It was a crisis by anybody's standards. How did we cope?

Out of frustration, the five men began to blame one another: "Why didn't you tell me how shallow it was?" complained Ned, who had been steering, to Hank, who had been watching the depth instrument.

"I said slow down, but you kept going!" countered Hank.

Then Charlie got after Rick: "It was your job to man the center-board winch! What happened?"

To which Rick defended himself: "I was! Andy [the captain] never told me to raise it."

They went around in a circle like this for several minutes, each pointing the finger at the other. Finally, I interrupted, asking, "Is there anything in this situation that is similar to how this team deals with crises back at the office?"

My question was met with a thoughtful pause. Charlie was the first to speak up: "This sounds *very* familiar! We have the damndest time ever learning what really happened when something goes wrong at the plant. Always this buck-passing!"

"What do others think? I invited the rest of the group to share their perceptions. No one spoke up. We sat in total silence for at least two minutes.

Finally, I broke the silence with another question, "Is it possible that we have not yet created enough safety with each other to have an open discussion about how mishaps occur? I wonder what it would take for us to feel easier about coming forth with what we know."

Andy, who had a closer relationship with Charlie than the others, spoke first, "I think some of us might be a little uneasy about how Charlie might react if we just stepped up and said, 'I screwed up.' I'm not talking about myself so much but . . . you know."

Rick and Ned nodded silently.

Hank agreed, "That's a problem for me, for sure. I don't like conflict. I want to look like I have it all under control. And I had a real strict father. Put that all together, and it adds up to one thing: *hiding when things go wrong.* Right now, I'm hoping no one will remember that I was the one who was watching the depth sounder!"

Everyone had a good laugh at Hank's disclosure. We needed something to break the tension.

The discussion that ensued focused on the lack of trust in the group. At first, people were tentative and polite, but as they warmed up, they became more direct.

At one point, someone asked Charlie how he would have reacted if this damage that we had just done to the sailboat had been done to a valuable piece of equipment back at the plant. Charlie acknowledged that his manner was often hotheaded and disrespectful in such cases. He couldn't help it, he said. He had put so much into building this company. It hurt him personally when anyone didn't care for it the way he did.

We all empathized with Charlie, and told him so, but at the same time his top team helped him see that people often avoided him because of his emotionally threatening style.

Fortunately, this sensitive topic was discussed in an atmosphere of care and concern for one another, and for the well-being of the company. Charlie was able to see himself as others saw him. But he was not willing to let things stop there. With my support, Charlie asked for everyone's help: "I need you to stand up to me if I'm going to learn to be more temperate in my judgments. I need people around me who will tell me that my behavior is threatening, and who can tell me, 'I'll give you the straight scoop if you'll respect me for speaking up.' I do respect people who speak up. I'm sorry my behavior doesn't always show it."

Lest we make Charlie the scapegoat of the day, I invited the others to look at how they, too, would like to change their own behavior so we could create a culture where bad news is learned from instead of suppressed. We each looked at how we had handled the crisis of running aground, using this incident as a mirror for seeing our characteristic reaction patterns.

Each man took his turn identifying how he had seen himself behaving in this crisis, how it was part of a familiar pattern for him, what he might need to learn in order to do certain things differently, and what kind of help he would like from other team members.

The discussion took place right there under the setting sun, waiting for the high tide, on empty stomachs, in full view of the gaping hole in the deck. When we finally had enough water under the boat to get it going again, the atmosphere in the group was entirely different than it had been that morning when we set sail.

There was good humor and a feeling of cooperation. There was attention to one another's needs and feelings. There was a cohesiveness that had not been there before.

Would this last? Would it translate into better working relationships? At the time, we did not know for sure. But I have worked with this group several times since then—never again on my sailboat, though!—and I'm pleased to report that the advances they made at their retreat have grown stronger with time.

When a team has survived rough waters together, or has run aground and then gotten free, or has met and mastered any significant challenge, it tends to be the stronger for it. In the case of Charlie and crew, the challenge was both physical (getting the boat free) and relational (learning what inhibited their free expression).

Solving problems together—learning together—is what builds team spirit. Storms and crises are not the only way. Often the shared experience of hashing out differences to arrive at a common vision or mission serves to bond individuals into a unit. Anytime a group works together to utilize or resolve differing inputs, this enhances the group's trust in its ability to solve future problems. Trust enables the group to put aside separative interests so they can solve problems collaboratively.

In Chapters Seven and Eight, we saw how respect for differences builds trust and how Both/And Thinking allows us to step back from a situation and see how all the parts interact to form a whole. In this chapter, we will expand on these themes, focusing on how a group of individuals develops into a high-performing team.

The primary vehicle for developing a team's learning capacity is what I call *group self-reflection,* that is, the capacity to listen and respond to feedback, both from the environment and from within the team's own ranks. In order to actually learn and create together, two other conditions must also be present: a sense of *shared purpose* and the ability of team members to communicate with one another in a way that *honors differing perspectives and talents.*

The group must feel that its mission is valid and useful, that the mission represents their personal values and purpose. This is not to say that everyone in the group must be polled before a team mission can be articulated; but everyone must have a chance to buy in, and to get a sense of how his or her contribution fits into the overall picture.

In a large organization, people need interactive mechanisms for connecting their personal purposes with the team purpose, and for connecting these with the overall corporate mission. This is usually done in the context of a group meeting or discussion. There are a variety of formats for conducting such group sessions.

The important ingredients in such a discussion are:

- the opportunity for people to hear the mission clearly stated in a way they can remember and relate to personally;
- the opportunity for people to ask questions and offer comment and to be heard and respected by management; and
- the opportunity to reflect together on how they felt about the meeting itself, about how effectively people worked together to meet their goals.

This last opportunity is critical if the group is to learn from how it does things and apply that learning to doing things better next time. This is an example of *group self-reflection.*

Carol Bartz, CEO of the highly successful Autodesk in Sausalito, California, conducts all group meetings with the aim of "making each person in the room feel that his or her contribution is absolutely essential for the success of the company. . . . I want people to leave that room feeling, 'This company couldn't do without me.'" This statement reveals Bartz's, and by extension Autodesk's, vision and values. Alongside the externally focused company mission, there is an equally important group-centered goal of creating unity through inclusion. The group's shared purpose addresses not only what they do for others, but also what they do for themselves— how to maintain a sense of unity, vitality, and commitment right here with one another.

When people feel valued, their commitment is strengthened. Think of some of the groups or relationships you have been part of. Does this idea fit with your experience? Other things being equal, has "feeling useful, valued, or needed" added to your sense of commitment to the relationship? I have observed the truth of this principle in a variety of settings from couple relationships to loosely affiliated boards of trustees. In working with couples, I have noticed a tendency in many people to hide their weaknesses in an attempt to win and keep the partner's love. Yet, in my in-depth study of one hundred couples, reported in *The Couple's Journey,* I found that partners are more likely to commit and stay in a relationship where they feel connected to one another through feeling useful, valued, or needed, rather than when they feel free of hassles. This principle holds true in work relationships as well. It is not our superficial "attractiveness" that bonds us to one another, but rather our need for one another.

Group Self-Reflection

Groups exist for two purposes: to get a *task* done; and to meet members' communal or *relational* needs, their needs to feel respected and valued. Anything the group does affects both of these aspects of group life.

In order for a group to learn from its experiences, it must have the capacity to reflect upon how well it is addressing both of these group purposes—the task and the relational. At least a few members need to be skilled at helping the group step back from what it is doing in order to observe itself.

Group self-reflection is not practiced very often in most organizations; and when it is, it is usually after a crisis. If we are to take change in stride rather than waiting for crises, we must learn and practice the art of ongoing self-observation. Are we clear about our task? Do our actions reflect clarity or confusion? Do we acknowledge and use each member's contribution?

One popular tool for group self-reflection is the Monday-morning-quarterback technique. The team sits down together after an event and looks back at how it did in order to share ideas about how to do better next time. We do not always need to wait until Monday morning to do our self-reflecting. We can sometimes do it right on the spot. And not all group self-reflection is about a single event. Often it concerns our ongoing efforts, or the activities of a particular subgroup, or our feelings about some group event.

Group self-reflection is to a group what self-awareness is to an individual. We observe ourselves, without blame or judgment, to see if what we are doing reflects our mission, values, and visions, and if our results reflect these aims. The capacity for ongoing self-reflection provides us with a continuous flow of feedback about how we are doing. This is how we learn from experience.

In the new workplace, it is important to reflect upon how closely our actions correspond to Learning/Discovery values:

- Are we able to anticipate the need for change when something isn't right?
- Do we embrace the unexpected?
- Is our intent to learn or to control?
- What is the trust level among group members?
- Do we communicate with respect?
- Do we seek to learn from those who see things differently from ourselves?

To become adept at group self-observation, a group needs mechanisms for seeing itself. If there are a few individuals in the group who understand how groups learn and change, these members can help the group create these mechanisms. To help your team, here is what you need to know:

1. How to see the group not as a collection of individuals, but in terms of the "group as a whole," as a system of interrelated individuals
2. How to track what the group is doing in terms of its *relational* aspect as well as its *task* aspect
3. How to help the group achieve consensus
4. How to trust and encourage the group's natural maturation or development from self-centeredness to synergy

1. Learning to View the Group as a Whole

Think of the groups you already participate in. You may belong to a family group, a work group, a church or community group, a school group, and one or more social groups. From your experience in each of these settings, you may already know something about group dynamics. *Group dynamics* refers to the body of knowledge that understands a group as a dynamic, ever-changing system. It is a system composed of interdependent parts, which both influence and are influenced by the whole. Your participation in your family group helps to shape how other members experience that family—whether it feels friendly or critical, relaxed or tense. And your belonging to this family definitely impacts you—

how you feel about yourself, how comfortable you feel with people, how you view the world, and how you behave in other social settings.

The two main components of teams as systems are *the individuals within the group* and *the group as a whole.* In describing the group as a whole, we use words like *atmosphere, morale, productivity, cohesiveness, synergy, and culture.* These are total-group characteristics. When doing a Monday-morning-quarterback session about a group you belong to, try looking at these total group characteristics. We all have the ability to perceive the group as a whole, but it is a skill that needs to be exercised and finely tuned if we are to fully tap our potential for learning and creating with others.

Group Personalities and Predicament

If you are fortunate enough to have several group experiences to draw upon, you may have noticed that groups have personalities of their own, just as individuals do. Some are efficiency-motivated, and some are more casual and laid back. Some are pragmatic, while others are idealistic. Some have a highly intellectual, thinking tone, while others are more feeling-oriented.

Groups also have needs, similar to an individual's needs—needs for a sense of efficacy and purpose, needs for feedback from the outside world, and even the need to be left alone at times.

Sometimes what the group needs for its learning and development may be at odds with what you, as an individual, need. You may need peace and harmony, but the group may need to confront an important conflict. Or you may need attention for some wounded feelings, while the group's primary need is to get on with the task at hand. This issue, the needs of the individual versus the needs of the group, is of course one of life's inescapable predicaments. When viewing the group as a whole, it is often useful to name the predicament that the group is presently wrestling with— such as how can we align individual needs with group goals? Or, how can we provide the right degree of structure or direction without making some members feel overcontrolled?

Group membership, and the fact that we often need to band with others in order to do things, engenders many predicaments like these. When we can step back and identify the predicament as a typical group problem that others have confronted before, we are empowered to deal with it more confidently.

Systems Thinking

When you view the group as a whole, you are using what organizational psychologists call "systems thinking." Any human system, such as the body, a family, or a work group, is composed of interrelated, interdependent parts. In a work group, the parts are the individual people. In the human body, the parts are your different organs, senses, cells, and structures. If one part of the system is weakened or disconnected from the whole, this will affect the other parts, too. Likewise, when something good happens to one part, this can have a beneficial effect on the whole system.

Think of your favorite athletic team or of an outstanding musical ensemble. What happens if one person in the group is having an off day? Usually, we would expect the performance of the entire group to suffer. But what if, when one person is out of sorts, everyone else works extra hard to compensate? What if each and every person feels 100 percent responsible for the team's success, not just for doing his or her share? Then the overall team performance does not need to suffer, because *the whole is greater than the sum of its parts*. This sense of shared responsibility occurs when trust is high in a system. Members are willing to go out on a limb for each other, to go above and beyond doing their fair share, trusting that if at some future time they are not performing up to par, someone will do the same for them.

A human system can be composed of two people, like a married couple or business partnership, five to ten people, like a family or work team, or hundreds or thousands of people, like a company or a municipality. The more people there are, the harder it will be to predict how a change in one part of the system will affect other parts. Still, when you belong to a system, your every action, no matter how small, will affect others. Once you accept this idea, you take responsibility for how your actions may affect others—even others whom you never see or with whom you feel no connection.

2. Attending to Both Task and Relational Needs

In reflecting on your past group experiences, you may have noticed how communication between members occurs at two levels at once. We are accomplishing some *task* or exchanging factual information. And we are meeting *relational* needs, such as the need to be recognized, or the need to feel useful.

In a family, for example, when the teenage daughter says to the father, "I won't be home until midnight," she is giving two levels of information. At the task level, she is giving her dad factual information about what time he can expect her. At the relational level she is communicating more than just the facts. If he is skillful at reading between the lines, he will notice that she did not ask him what time to be home. She told him. She has communicated something about the power relationship between father and daughter: that she is now setting her own curfew.

The relational level of a communication is always received, whether we are conscious of it or not. The father may be upset and not realize exactly why: "It was just something about her tone, about the way she said it that made me uncomfortable."

To learn from group self-reflection, it is important to know what the group is doing at both the task level and the relational level because task accomplishment depends on the degree of trust in the relationship. Trust is built at the relational level. It is not enough to agree on who will do what. Conditions in the group as a whole must be such that people feel good about working together and feel some ownership for the task. The highest-quality solutions are of little value if they won't be implemented in a high-quality way. So we must use our group self-reflection skills to assess what is going on "between the lines" (at the relational level) that could sabotage trust. In doing this, we bring the subconscious into consciousness—where it can be managed consciously.

Let's take an example: A group decides to use a new system for tracking customer complaints. During the decision-making process, three members repeatedly bring up concerns about the new procedure. Their concerns are addressed by a spokesperson for the majority opinion. The explanations are done in a one-way, information-only style. They do not attend to the dissenters' fears, and they do not inquire whether these three members feel that their concerns have been addressed. At the task level, the explanation is accurate and informative. On the relational level, here is what the three dissenters hear: "We don't have time for your concerns. They are not important enough to be taken seriously. Be quiet, and get with the program." The three leave the meeting feeling disrespected and invalidated.

A few weeks later, it is discovered that the new procedures are not being used by these three key people. Upon investigation, it is determined that they did not see the need for the change and felt alienated and excluded during the decision-making process.

Such communication breakdowns are commonplace. Often, they go undetected, but their costs are enormous. They can easily be prevented, however, if we get into the habit of reflecting on our own behavior—looking for problems we should be addressing instead of denying problems and being rudely awakened by a crisis. To prevent problems such as the one described here with these three dissenting members, there are a number of things other group members, or the leader, might do:

Watch for any type of tension or slowdown, for evidence that some members are upset or preoccupied. These could manifest as a member's silence or withdrawal, remarks that show anger or irritation, a tendency for one or two members to dominate, several members drifting off on a tangent, low energy or lack of engagement with the task, prolonged conflict-laden interchanges.

When any of these are noted, comment in a friendly, nonaccusing manner about what you observe. Be careful not to do this in a way that singles out one person as the problem or in a way that might publicly embarrass someone. Here are some examples of ways to do this:

When one member has been silent: "Sally, you have been looking thoughtful. If you feel like sharing what's on your mind, I'd like to hear it."

When most members have been silent and only a few have been participating, or when one or two have been dominating: "I'd like to summarize what has been said so far, and then I'd like to hear what Karen, Ron, and Herb have been thinking."

When someone is angry or irritated: "Let me see if I have heard your concern, Joe, is it that _____?" (Restate what Joe has just said in a way that shows empathy for his feelings.)

When the group's energy is flagging (evidenced by slumped postures, lack of eye contact, distractibility): First, identify what you are feeling. If you are bored or confused, you can use this feeling as part of your "process observation." Then you might comment: "I'm confused about where we are going. Does anyone else share this feeling?"

When people seem to be drifting away from the agenda: "It sounds to me like we're getting into some areas that we hadn't planned on for this meeting. I'd like to go back to what we were discussing earlier. I have an idea I'd like your comments on _____." (Then you present an idea that relates to something that was discussed earlier when the group was focused on the agreed-upon agenda.)

When two or a few members have been engaged in prolonged conflict: "It would be helpful to me to learn how others feel about this issue." Then look around the room, asking, "How does everyone else feel?"

From these examples, it should be clear that your own feelings about what is going on are the best barometer of what others may be feeling. When you intervene in a task-oriented discussion to offer an observation on relational issues, you will be received most easily if you stick with your own feelings rather than trying to interpret the group's behavior. People have a tendency to feel judged, and therefore resistant, when someone interprets their behavior.

The ability to spot feelings and relational needs that are being overlooked is an invaluable skill. Groups and organizations are notorious for overlooking the human factor in the quest for efficiency. Yet as we have seen over and over, long-term efficiency is best served by attending to peoples' feelings as well as to the task.

Here is another example of a group meeting where two levels of communication are occurring at once:

Lisa and Marlon are codirectors of a large nonprofit educational institution. In a meeting with their administrative staff and board of directors, the subject of next year's budget is being discussed. There is a cloud of tension in the room, but people plod along pretending that everything's just fine. You notice that Lisa and Marlon have not looked at each other all morning, and only speak about one another in the third person, never addressing the other directly, even though they are seated on opposite sides of a circular conference table. The discussion has no life in it. People seem to be saying what they think others want to hear. It appears that no one wants to rock the boat. You are uncomfortable. What could you do that might be of help to the group? Let's look at your options.

If you want to learn and help your team learn, you will have to risk making some people uncomfortable. To help you in this, you need to feel that your sense of self is not dependent on others' approval. You need to place *making yourself* at a higher priority than *protecting yourself.* Recall the work you began in Chapter Six in this regard. If your goal is to help your team, you may have to momentarily put aside your need to be liked and focus on what is good for the group as a whole. The best way to use your discomfort constructively is to reflect on your own feelings about what is going on: "This is such an important discussion. I wonder why we aren't more animated. The atmosphere in here feels blunted. Does anyone else notice this?"

This is a risk. Of course, it becomes less of a risk if the group is already committed to learning from this sort of feedback. Most teams have not learned how to be self-reflective in this way. As a result, they cannot see when their actions are contrary to their goals.

Often a team needs a good organizational consultant to teach its members how to be self-reflective. A consultant can show members how to stand outside of the group momentarily in order to observe what the group is doing and why. She can reveal the defensive communication patterns the group may be stuck in. And she can lead you in problem-solving discussions aimed at creating new norms that are more conducive to team learning.

Norms that promote team learning are the same norms that foster individual learning in organizations: safety, honesty, respect, and the desire to achieve mutual understanding. In addition, it is very important to get group agreement on the value of group self-reflection.

In my own consulting work, many of the groups who have made

a commitment to learning and self-understanding have adopted one or more of the following practices designed to foster an awareness of the relational level of group life:

1. Some groups appoint a rotating group observer, a member charged with the task of watching for situations when the relationships and feelings in the group seem to be interfering with the achievement of the task. This member is allowed to stop the action anytime during the discussion with observations on the group's behavior.

2. Some groups set aside ten minutes at the end of every team meeting to reflect as a group on such questions as:

- Did we stay focused on our purpose?
- Did everyone get a chance to contribute?
- Was the tone friendly or contentious?
- How do we feel about what we accomplished and how we went about doing it?

Using such questions over a period of time builds the group's ability to be self-reflective.

3. Sometimes a group will decide to break into two subgroups in the middle of a difficult discussion. One subgroup forms a circle and sits inside of the other subgroup. The inner group actively engages in a continuation of the discussion. The outer group observes. After a while, the groups switch places. After both groups have been in the inner circle for approximately equal periods of time, the two groups share observations on what they saw using the questions listed in practice 2 above.

These tools can be used with groups of any size or sophistication level. People see a lot more than they admit. Usually, because there is no group agreement on the value of self-observation, we pretend we don't see these things. Some members may be afraid that they are the only ones who see them. Once permission is given to see and comment on the subtler dynamics of group performance, and we realize we are not alone, it's amazing how observant everyone is!

Group Action Research

Related to the ability to step outside of the flow of content so we can observe the group's relational activity during a meeting is the equally important ability to step back and evaluate ourselves more generally: Does everyone have a clear idea of our shared purpose? How well are we structured to meet our purpose? Do team members feel their contributions are valued? Do we reward what we say we value? How well have we aligned individual needs and talents with team goals? How well are we adapting to changes in the marketplace? How do we feel about the quality of our products and services?

Occasionally, it is useful for a group to assess its own effectiveness using an action research approach. In action research, we individually survey or interview team members on the same set of questions. Then the person collecting these responses summarizes the data so it can be reported back to the group. Next we convene to see how everyone responded, and to see what problems this reveals. Then we engage as a group in problem-solving around the issues needing attention.

All groups, teams, and organizations need procedures to help them look at themselves and learn from what they observe. Even if a trained organization consultant is needed to get such a program started, the consultant can teach you some methods to use on your own so that you can learn to be your own "consultant."

3. How to Help Your Team Reach Consensus

Whether you are in a position of formal leadership or not, it is important to understand the consensus-building process. Every team member needs to feel responsible for what happens in the group. In the new workplace, there is no us and them. It's all us.

Building consensus requires commitment and effort from everyone on the team. It is a process of mutual trust-building and learning. To help move your group from divergent interests to unified action, you need to attend to several aspects of group life:

1. Is there a consensus-building procedure in place in this group? Does it have a history of consensus decision-making?
2. How well do people know, respect, and trust one another? Do they know each other's strengths? Do people feel safe enough to admit limitations?

3. How diverse are the styles and interests of group members?
4. How much time do we have for discussion and dialogue—for deeply listening to one another?
5. How skilled are the members in communicating and listening?
6. Are there some members who can hold in mind the needs of the group as a whole?
7. How does the group manage conflict? Does it have a history of facing and resolving it, or of avoiding it?
8. What are the norms and expectations about group self-reflection?
9. Does the group have a fallback mechanism for decision-making if it cannot reach consensus?

Different group members will have different things to contribute to the process of reaching consensus and taking action. Some will be more task-oriented and will be good at coming up with ideas and keeping the group focused on the task. Some will be more relationship-oriented and can offer support, encouragement, and acknowledgment. Some will be comfortable with conflict and differences and will be helpful to the group when a hidden conflict needs to be surfaced. Others who may be less comfortable with conflict can help defuse tension through seeking harmony or common ground.

The following checklist summarizes the various functions needed to achieve sufficient agreement to take action. As you read the list, check those functions that you do naturally, and note which are more difficult for you. Notice also if any of these vital functions are missing in any of your groups. When a function is absent, the group needs to become aware of it and appoint or train someone to fill this role.

Functions Needed to Build Consensus

Task functions:
_____setting the agenda or goal
_____initiating new topics for discussion
_____asking for agreement or disagreement
_____clairfying points of agreement or disagreement
_____pointing out factual disagreements or differing assumptions

_____seeking or giving information or opinions

_____suggesting alternatives

_____organizing data

_____coordinating (keeping discussion focused or relevant to the task)

_____clarifying

_____summarizing

_____testing for consensus ("Are we all in agreement that _____? What do we need in order to be ready to take action?")

Relational functions:

_____supporting and encouraging

_____defusing conflict

_____raising awareness of disrespectful behaviors

_____looking for common ground

_____suggesting useful communication tools (e.g., active listening)

_____suggesting helpful group rituals (e.g., a period of shared silence)

_____giving feedback

_____keeping communication channels open within the group

_____keeping conversation flow moving, or restarting it when blocked

_____surfacing hidden conflicts or other blocks to consensus

_____helping members notice when they are focused on learning versus control

An often-overlooked function in groups is that of testing for consensus. Too often, you will assume there is consensus because everyone who is speaking up seems to be in accord. Only later does the group learn that some people will not jump into a discussion unless they are specifically polled. You might invite them in, saying, "What do others think about this?" or "What do you think, Marge?" It is dangerous to assume agreement without testing for it.

Another common problem in consensus-building is seeking unanimous agreement too early—before the group has aired its concerns or before there is sufficient trust or alignment. Testing is okay, but be careful not to put covert pressure on people. If there is real time pressure, and there often is, mention this explicitly, but be mindful of the tendency some people have to conform under pressure and then to resent or resist later on.

Remember that agreeing to disagree is often good enough. The decision reached can still be called a consensus of the group, even if there is not unanimous agreement. A group has reached consensus if there is enough agreement to allow the group to take action. The important factor in determining whether the dissenters will support the decision is their feeling that their views have been respected. It helps to state explicitly that we are agreeing to disagree and to acknowledge the minority for their willingness to cooperate.

Building consensus requires careful attention to the relational level of group life. Here are some other ways to help your group communicate better so it can achieve consensus:

1. If the process takes longer than you feel it should, don't give up. Put the question to the group, "Why is this process so laborious?" This will get opposing sides thinking together about something.

2. If the group is split into two factions around an issue, suggest the pro-and-then-con technique that I used with my client, the paper-manufacturing company, discussed in Chapter Eight.

3. If the tone is contentious, suggest this *group active-listening* technique: After someone speaks, the next speaker has to summarize what the previous speaker said (to her satisfaction) before offering his contribution.

4. Appoint one group member to be the consensus-tester/summarizer for the group. This person "plays back the tape" (summarizes) from time to time to see if others agree that this is where the group has come so far. Then she asks if there is consensus yet, and if there is not, she asks, "What do we need to do at this point to reach consensus?"

5. Pay attention to the level of trust in the group. Encourage people to be open and respectful about their differences. This builds a feeling that "this is a place where I can be myself." If trust is low, don't push for agreement. Take time for listening to each other. Suggest that as we listen, our intent is to learn from each other, not to change each other's minds.

4. Encouraging the Group's Natural Developmental Process

Groups and teams, like the individuals who populate them, have an inborn need to learn and expand their capacities. If you understand the stages that a team tends to go through as it matures into a high-performing unit, you can help your team move through these stages more consciously.

To help you understand how a group "grows up" over time, think of the analogy of how an individual grows up. First, as a baby, you are pretty dependent on others and not very resourceful. At this stage, you need a lot of attention from adults. As you get bigger, you find more and more things you can do for yourself. But you still need adult guidance to help you know if you are doing things right. Then, as an adolescent, you want the freedom to do things your own way, and even to make your own mistakes—so you can learn to take care of yourself. When you reach early adulthood, you have mastered certain life skills, but you are still in a pretty steep learning curve. You have earned a certain autonomy, but you also need others' feedback and support to help you become all that you can be. Finally, in later adulthood, you are focused, not so much on improving yourself, but on giving back to the world from what you have learned.

If we apply this analogy to a group or team as a living, growing organism, we see five stages that a group passes through from infancy to maturity. At Stage 1, group members are dependent on some outside authority or on a group leader to tell them why they exist as a group. Members need to know "Why are we here as a group?" and "Why am I in this group?" Members need support from someone in authority (the adult) to help them define their reason for being.

At Stage 2, members are less dependent on the authority (leader, management directive, mandate from external environment) for their sense of purpose. But they now need some guidance or structure to help them establish agreed-upon roles and procedures. "Who is responsible for what?" and "How will we work together?" become the central questions.

At Stage 3, the group develops the ability to take action as a unit. Similar to the adolescent, sometimes its actions are appropriate to its purpose, and sometimes not. There is a fair degree of trial and error at this stage. This is the time when it is most important for the "adults" (management, team leader) to let go of control. This can also be the time when it is hardest to do this—because the group is still divided within itself and not as trustworthy as the adults might wish. But if the group is to continue to mature, it needs to work out its internal conflicts and ineptitudes without too much outside control.

At Stage 4, the group's main focus is on being productive and on learning ways to continually improve performance. It has developed ways for dealing with differences and disagreements that do not detract from getting the task done. It continues to learn and grow through confronting internal conflicts and external challenges.

At Stage 5, the group is still focused on being productive, but now it must also look at how to respond to changing conditions in the outside world or to the changing needs of its members—how to revamp its purpose or revitalize itself.

As a group develops, it needs less outside leadership and more opportunity for self-management. But in order to become self-managing, most groups need some training or guidance regarding how to work as a team (how to negotiate roles, how to make decisions, how to build consensus). The team leader, if there is one, needs to let go of control more and more as the team learns to work together. But most people need to feel that "someone cares." So it is important that someone continue to pay attention to giving the team positive feedback when it achieves a goal and support (listening, resources) when it expresses a need.

As a team develops, it can handle more conflict and diversity. Greater group strength and cohesion pave the way for greater tolerance of individual differences and individual freedom. When your team is in its infancy, you need to manage potential conflicts carefully so people don't feel too threatened. At this early stage, a team leader may need to do some *harmonizing*—emphasizing the common ground between two divergent views. Later on, you can afford to sit back and let people "have at it" a bit more.

As a team's self-management capabilities grow, team members' functions tend to differentiate based on individual interests and abilities. Someone will become the team "accountant," another the "quality control person," another the "new ideas person," and so forth. Most people will wear more than one hat. It takes time to discover the best fit between individual talents and team needs. As the group continues to grow, it will develop more effective ways of coordinating these different functions. At first, coordination might occur in team meetings. Later on, information needed by different individuals might be routed via informal channels, allowing for fewer meetings.

With increasing maturity, task-relevant feedback between members becomes more open and spontaneous. At first, it may be useful to install structured methods for exchanging feedback. Jerry Brandt, president of Interface Systems in Alamo, California, convenes his team once a month during the early phases of the group's life for "barnacle-cleaning sessions," where people are led through a series of structured exercises designed to surface and resolve hidden conflicts and misunderstandings. Later on, people can be trusted to do this on their own on an as-needed basis. Sometimes, more mature groups still need structured rituals for barnacle-cleaning, but perhaps not as frequently. With time, people feel safer to express feelings, to debate controversial issues, and to experiment. They also develop more concern for others and are more able to listen and build upon one another's ideas.

More highly developed groups function more as a unit, both in how they work and in how they feel. When something good happens, they all feel good together. Likewise, when something disappointing happens, they share a sense of loss.

Some groups develop into a cohesive unit rather quickly. Others take much longer. If you want to assist your team to develop as rapidly as it can, refer often to this overview of the basic developmental tasks that need to be accomplished by groups as they grow from dependency to independence to interdependence.

This chart summarizes the five stages of team development, emphasizing what the group needs to learn at each stage and what you as member or leader need to pay special attention to at various points in order to encourage team learning. As we consider the issues that surface at each stage, you will notice that there are both task needs and relational needs every step of the way. Often the task-oriented issues mask the deeper feeling or relational needs. So be sure and watch for both types of needs when you look at what the group is trying to do at each stage.

The Five Stages of Team Development

Stage I
The Inclusion/Identity Stage

WHAT TEAM NEEDS TO LEARN: Why are we here?

TASK LEVEL: Members need a sense of group's purpose.

RELATIONAL LEVEL: Members need a sense of belonging or inclusion.

HOW TO FOSTER TEAM LEARNING: Invite members to comment on their sense of the group's purpose, and help each person feel recognized and needed in relation to that purpose.

Stage II
The Rules and Roles Stage

WHAT TEAM NEEDS TO LEARN: What is expected of me/us?

TASK LEVEL: Who is responsible for what? What are our standards of performance and governing procedures?

RELATIONAL LEVEL: Will I be able to do what is expected? Will I be valued for my contribution?

HOW TO FOSTER TEAM LEARNING: Develop agreed-upon procedures for decision-making, delegation, and evaluation.

Stage III
The Action-Taking Stage

WHAT TEAM NEEDS TO LEARN: How to take action as a unit.

TASK LEVEL: Best ways to achieve our purpose.

The Five Stages of Team Development (con't.)

RELATIONAL LEVEL: How to manage differences in style and values. Members need to feel their uniqueness is recognized.

HOW TO FOSTER TEAM LEARNING: Encourage and make it safe to express divergent views and novel ideas.

Stage IV
The Self-Monitoring Stage

WHAT TEAM NEEDS TO LEARN: Confidence in its ability to act as a unit and to continually create better ways to achieve the team's purpose.

TASK LEVEL: Developing new and better procedures and policies.

RELATIONAL LEVEL: How to be open to feedback from within the group and from outside.

HOW TO FOSTER TEAM LEARNING: Ask self-reflective questions that also promote a sense of unity by using words like "our" and "we," such as "Does this further our team goals?" and "Are we all in agreement on this?"

Stage V
The Creativity/Continual Renewal Stage

WHAT TEAM NEEDS TO LEARN: Why continue? What's next? Do we need a new reason for being or a change in structure?

TASK LEVEL: Devise ways of changing or adapting the group's purpose in response to feedback from the company or the marketplace.

RELATIONAL LEVEL: Am I still needed here? What do
I need to let go of to continue
to develop with this group?

HOW TO FOSTER TEAM LEARNING: Create conversations and rituals
to help people let go of the old
to make room for the new.
Celebrate accomplishments.
Critique mistakes. Summarize
what we have learned together.

You can use this five-stage map to stimulate group self-reflective discussions or to raise the group's awareness of the issue they are wrestling with. This helps the group become more conscious, and therefore in charge, of its typically unconscious maturation process. When a group becomes more conscious of the developmental task it is attempting to complete, it can perform this task more effectively—with the entire membership sharing responsibility for the group's maturation.

Having an overview of how groups learn and change over time will assist you in seeing the group as a whole. Some tasks will be appropriate for the early stages. Other tasks cannot be accomplished until more trust has developed.

Meta-Skill Builder 37:
How Groups Change over Time

Think of a group you have belonged to, and step back far enough to view the group as a whole system. Describe your assessment of the group in terms of such total group characteristics as atmosphere, cooperation among members, and trust. Reflect also on how the character of the group changed over time as the group "got to know itself better." How did its character change as it matured? Was it better able to accomplish certain tasks at one stage as compared to another? Which tasks seemed to be best done early in the group's life, and which were more easily accomplished later on?

Every group or team that wishes to become continuously self-renewing must have the ability to give itself feedback and the ability to accept feedback from the environment. In order to learn from this feedback, team members need to have a sense of themselves as part of the group as a whole.

How Being a Team Learner Can Make You Indispensable to Your Organization and Customers

1. Blocks to group effectiveness often appear to come from the personality problems of individuals, from the fact that these are "difficult people," when in fact there is often a group dynamic operating in these cases as well. When you are a team learner, you know how to work with such a problem as a system problem as well as an individual problem.

If you treat only the individual who seems to be causing the problem, and do nothing about the group's unmet needs, it won't be long before someone else will come forth to act out the same disturbing behavior. The systems approach leads to a sense of shared responsibility by the entire group. It also leads to more lasting solutions because everyone contributes to the solution, and everyone learns in the process. This empowers team members to see the complexity of group problems rather than resorting to simplistic reactions like scapegoating or blaming. Your ability to demonstrate this degree of sophistication in problem-solving makes you a valuable teacher for others.

2. When you understand what the group is trying to do at the relational level as well as at the task level, you can assist the group in identifying the subtler forces at work that can help or hinder progress on the task. This is a relatively rare skill in today's organization—and one that is essential to helping your team do its job better.

3. When you understand the stages of development that groups go through, you can help the group become more aware of what it must do to get where it wants to go. Again, this skill is relatively rare and can position you for leadership roles that most people are not equipped to handle.

4. Your ability to view the group as a whole enables you to mirror back to the others the ways in which seemingly conflicting

ideas and styles actually complement one another when seen in context. This enhances your ability to lead the group in managing conflicts and differences.

How Being a Team Learner Can Help You Prevent or Respond to Crisis

1. As power and authority are decentralized in the workplace, more and more work will be done in small, autonomous groups or teams. Thus, it becomes increasingly important to understand small-group dynamics so you can help your group take decisive action. In a crisis, you cannot afford to waste time in indecision or impasse.

2. If you are undergoing personal crisis in response to some external crisis, it helps to have the support of a caring community of friends and colleagues. Your ability to work as a team player cements your relationships with your community. This can give you the confidence you need to make deep personal changes.

And Remember...

- Groups depend for their vitality on a shared sense of belonging and trust. If this is missing, if some members feel they are not needed and respected by the group, these members will create a drain on the group's resources.
- A shared sense of purpose is also vital. Without this, unnecessary conflicts impede the group's ability to take action.
- Some conflict is unavoidable in a diverse group. Groups need mechanisms for surfacing, resolving, and learning from differences. Until a group has developed such mechanisms, it will be hampered in its ability to make decisions or take action.
- If a group is to continually grow in its effectiveness, some of its members need to lead the rest of the group in reflecting on whether the group culture is supportive of its stated mission.

How the Six Meta-Skills Support and Build on One Another

When you can participate with the change process, you understand that change occurs stage by stage, and that letting go of something you no longer need leaves an opening for something new and more appropriate. So Meta-Skill 1, Participate with Change, paves the way for Meta-Skill 2, Let Go.

The ability to let go of your attachment to how things should be makes it easier to see and relate to things as they really are, to focus on essences over appearances. This makes it easier to see yourself more deeply and truly, to Focus on Essentials, Meta-Skill 3.

When you are grounded in your essential self, your communications with others naturally feel more connected. You relate heart-to-heart, person-to-person, not role-to-role or function-to-function. You care about the person inside the role. This allows you to Communicate to Build Trust, Meta-Skill 4.

The ability to form relationships in which respect for each person's uniqueness is the highest value prepares you to use Meta-Skill 5, Both/And Thinking, both in your interpersonal relationships and in creative problem-solving.

And finally, if you are to be a Team Learner, Meta-Skill 6, you need to have the other five meta-skills well integrated into your repetoire. Teams change and develop, so you need to understand the rhythms and cycles of change, and to be able to help the team let go of what no longer serves its mission. To be a fully functioning team member, you need the commitment and vitality that comes when you are expressing your essence in your work. To build group support for your ideas, and to help your team arrive at consensus, you need to be able to communicate with others in ways that build trust. In order to make use of each member's contribution to the team, to help each person feel valued, and to resolve conflicts, Both/And Thinking is vitally important.

All six strategic meta-skills are vehicles to help you get from an overconcern with Security/Control values to an openness to deep, ongoing learning. There will always be a natural tension between the need to control people or situations and the need to be open to learning from them. Working with this tension is a natural part of life. It is part of what gives a life its vitality and character. Each of us will strike a different balance between these two polar forces —control versus openness to learning. And in different situations, we will come out in different places on the control-learning continuum.

While we must all learn to be better learners, we must also beware of the tendency to judge or blame ourselves or anyone else who is not as open as we might wish. Let's see if we can be open to learning in a way that includes learning from others who may not be as open as we.

PART THREE

Leading
YOUR
ORGANIZATION
toward
LEARNING/
DISCOVERY

CHAPTER TEN

Joining Forces with Your Organization

If we want our workplaces to support our aliveness, we must help our organizations develop the capacity for continuous self-renewal. Organizations need to learn how to "make themselves while making a living," just as individuals do.

You will need the support of your organization if you are going to become a Learning/Discovery thinker. Some organizational cultures are truly engaged in ongoing learning, and some only pay lip service to this ideal. If you have a commitment to Learning/Discovery, you can help your organization—so it can, in turn, help you.

If an organization is to make the transition to Learning/Discovery, it must be structured so that it supports and rewards employees who

- perceive the need for change and innovation;
- admit and learn from productive failures;
- let go of the need to appear single-handedly in control;
- bring essential values like honesty and fairness into their work;
- communicate respectfully;
- foster Both/And thinking; and
- harness the energy and wisdom of the group or team.

One way you can help your organization is by acknowledging and rewarding the people and groups you work with when they demonstrate any of these abilities. You can also be on the lookout for organizational habit patterns that block learning. Remember, change occurs not from pushing against resistance but from removing the blocks to change.

Let's start by looking at the present situation in your organization without judgment or blame. That's the first stage in the eight-stage process described in Chapter Four. Then we will consider some things you can do to foster organizational learning.

To effectively incorporate the six Learning/Discovery meta-skills into your life at work, you need to do the following:

1. Realistically assess your organization's ability to practice Learning/Discovery values
2. Envision yourself consistently and effectively embodying the Learning/Discovery attitude
3. Create a support system of people and groups who share your commitment to learning

1. Assessing Your Organization

How well does your organization really understand Learning/Discovery thinking? Which aspects of the organization's culture already embody this view? Where can you expect to encounter resistance?

In setting out to answer these questions, imagine yourself as a cultural anthropologist entering a culture whose folkways and rituals are different from yours. As a cultural anthropologist, you do not judge or belittle what you see. You know that every aspect of culture has some function.

This posture will help you remain objective. It is your job to discover the function of each habit pattern your encounter. Your goal is to learn all you can about how people do things here, and why they do things as they do.

At first, you may feel somewhat critical of those aspects of the culture that seem foreign to you. Such criticalness usually reveals your own fear. If you are feeling critical, consider what fears might be coming up for you. Perhaps you fear that you may be criticized for your Learning/ Discovery values—so the best defense is a good offense. Or perhaps you fear getting no response at all. Note the fear, and use it as important information about your own resistances to change. We all have resistances, so it's best to acknowledge them. Otherwise, they are suppressed and influence our behavior in ways we cannot see.

As a Learning/Discovery anthropologist, you are sincerely interested in understanding the unwritten code of conduct of this organization, particularly the degree to which it embodies Learning/Discovery versus Security/Control thinking.

You want to learn, for example, if it is safe admitting to a superior that you don't know something—or are you likely to be labeled incompetent?

You want to find out how management deals with "bad news." Do they shoot the messenger or commend his forthrightness?

You want to know how differences and disagreements are dealt with, and the extent to which people treat one another respectfully. Is it usual for people to communicate face-to-face when they have an issue to be resolved, or do they use indirect methods like memos, gossiping, or talking via each person's supervisor?

To assess your organization's learning and discovery "quotient," let's examine six key areas of organizational life, corresponding to the six strategic meta-skills discussed in Part Two. What are the unwritten rules of conduct in this culture regarding

- recognizing the need for change and rectifying problems in the system?
- admitting the need for outside help or input?
- encouraging or discouraging the expression of each person's uniqueness?
- communicating respectfully, in ways that promote trust?
- respecting and using differences in perspective?
- rewarding group consciousness rather than individualism?

Meta-Skill Builder 38:
Give Your Organization This Test

Here are twenty-four multiple-choice questions, four for each of the six meta-skills. Choose the item (a, b, c, or d) that most closely describes the climate in your organization. Pay no attention to the numbers in parentheses after each item. These numbers will be explained in the section "Scoring Procedure."

How Well Does Your Organization Participate with Change? (Items 1–4)

1. If a customer has a complaint about a product or service, is it company policy to

a. listen to the customer's ideas about how to do it better? (1)
b. empower the employee who receives the complaint to take action to satisfy the customer? (3)
c. ask the customer to send a letter to the customer relations department? (0)

2. If someone in sales receives repeated complaints about the company's hot new product, is this salesperson most likely to

a. deal with the complaint and then forget about it? (2)
b. deal with the complaint and then report it to her manager? (3)
c. complain to coworkers about how hard it is to sell this product? (0)

3. Is a major organizational change more apt to be driven by

a. a crisis that has been brewing for a while, but which has gone unheeded? (0)
b. sensing a coming change in internal needs or the external environment? (2)
c. the projection of possible changes in the environment that have not yet materialized? (2)
d. a combination of b and c? (3)

4. Does your organization have any sort of transition-monitoring team or mechanism in place? If so, rate its effectiveness on a scale of 1 to 10:

a. 1 to 3 (1)
b. 4 to 7 (2)

c. 8 to 10 (3)
d. No such mechanism exists in the organization. (0)

To What Extent Can Your Organization Let Go of Its Need to Appear in Control? (Items 5–8)

5. If your chief competitor launches a new product that threatens to take market share, is it the practice in your organization to

a. get your R&D department to develop a close approximation of this product without a thorough study of the competitor's product? (1)
b. study the competitor's product, then come out with a product that is significantly superior to your competitor's, even if it takes several months longer than the course of action suggested in option a? (3)
c. increase sales and marketing efforts for your existing products? (0)

6. How often does top management ask (sincerely) for ideas from lower levels in the organization?

a. often (3)
b. rarely (1)
c. never (0)

7. How often does top management, or any manager, admit uncertainty or error?

a. often (3)
b. rarely (1)
c. never (0)

8. What is likely to happen to you if you need more help on a project than your manager thinks you are going to need?

a. You won't mention this for fear of the repercussions. You will do the project as best you can without any outside help. (0)
b. You will go to your manager and ask for the help you need. (3)
c. You will find the help you need on your own (2)

How Well Does Your Organization Encourage Expression of Employees' Essential Selves? (Items 9–12)

9. To what extent does the performance appraisal system encourage people to set their own objectives for further personal and professional development?

a. not at all (0)
b. to some extent, depending on the individual manager (1)
c. to a great extent (3)

10. In your estimation, what proportion of employees feel like they are expressing some of their own personal passion through their job?

a. most (3)
b. between 25 and 75 percent (2)
c. very few (1)

11. If you went to your manager to talk about redesigning your job so that you could do more of the things you enjoy, what outcome would be most likely?

a. My manager would look at me as if I were crazy. (0)
b. My manager would explore ideas and solutions with me. (3)
c. My manager would get to work and redesign my job for me. (0)

12. How much direction and control do managers exercise after delegating a piece of work?

a. Usually, they tell you the results they want and let you achieve that result in your own way. (2)
b. They tell you the result that they want. Then they ask about how you plan to achieve that result. Then they give you feedback on your ideas. (3)
c. They tell you the result they want and then spell out how they would like it to be done. (0)

How Well Does Your Organization Encourage Respectful Communication? (Items 13—16)

13. What proportion of the workforce receives training in communication and feedback skills?

a. less than half (0)
b. about 40 to 60 percent (2)
c. more than 60 percent (3)

14. How would you rate your immediate work group in terms of respectful behavior (on a scale from 1 to 10)?

a. 1 to 3 (0)
b. 4 to 7 (1)
c. 8 to 10 (3)

15. If one person treats another disrespectfully during a group meeting, what consequences are most likely (based on your experience)?

a. People ignore it. (0)
b. There is a built-in process for learning from such instances. (3)
c. Someone will give the person feedback about it. (2)

16. What are the norms in your organization about expressing negative feelings, such as anger, hurt or disappointment?

a. People are expected to manage these feelings by themselves without expressing them. (1)
b. Certain managers or members of the top echelon are allowed to express whatever they feel as impulsively as they like, and they do so. (0)
c. Both a and b are true. (0)
d. We have agreed-upon feedback processes that we use to clear the air. (3)

To What Extent Does Your Organization Model Both/And Thinking? (Items 17—20)

17. What is management's style of dealing with differing perceptions or interests?

a. There are agreed-upon processes for managing differences that are used and that work well most of the time. (3)
b. There are processes for managing differences, but no one uses them. (1)
c. There is an attitude equivalent to "may the best person win" (whoever is "stronger" wins). (0)
d. No one pays much attention to how differences are managed. (0)

18. How might an employee at a lower echelon get the attention of top management regarding an issue of vital importance to the company?

a. The employee would either write or call to make an appointment to speak with someone on the top team. (3)
b. The employee's concern would be screened by an administrative aide before an appointment would be granted. (1)
c. While there may be procedures for doing this, very few would ever even consider it. (0)

19. What proportion of your workforce has access to training in diversity issues?

a. less than half (0)
b. about 40 to 60 percent (2)
c. more than 60 percent (3)

20. What proportion of your workforce has access to training in conflict resolution, mediation, or win-win negotiating?

a. less than half (0)
b. about 40 to 60 percent (2)
c. more than 60 percent (3)

How Well Does Your Organization Help Employees Become Team Learners? (Items 21–24)

21. How often do you attend meetings where group members consciously reflect together about how the meeting went after it is over (or during it)?

a. none (0)
b. occasionally (2)
c. often (3)

22. What proportion of your workforce has access to training in group leadership, meeting facilitation, or group-process skills?

a. less than half (0)
b. about 40 to 60 percent (2)
c. more than 60 percent (3)

23. How successful is your organization in providing tangible rewards for team accomplishments in a way that encourages people to share information and resources?

a. not at all (0)
b. somewhat (1)
c. pretty successful (3)

24. Are there mechanisms in place whereby personal status is enhanced by providing others with help or knowledge?

a. If there are, no one pays attention to them. (0)
b. There are, but they do not have the desired result. (1)
c. Yes, and they are effective to some degree. (3)

Scoring Procedure

Notice the numbers 0, 1, 2, or 3, in parentheses at the end of each possible answer above. These numbers indicate the value to be given for each option. Give your organization 0, 1, 2, or 3 points, depending upon which option you selected. Add up the total number of points to get a composite score. The highest possible composite score is 72. You can also get a score for each of the six categories. The highest possible category scores are as follows:

Change: 12
Letting Go: 12
Essence: 12
Communication: 12

Both/And: 12
Team: 12

If your organization's composite score was below 50, or if any category scores were below 8, it probably is not very friendly toward Learning/Discovery thinking. In the next section, we will consider some things you can do right where you are in the organization to begin to promote Learning/Discovery.

Remember, you do not have to occupy a formal leadership position in order to have a positive, and significant, impact. If our organizations are to survive and self-renew, we must all become leaders now, no matter what our position in the organization. In fact, if we want to be valued and supported by our organizations, we need to become leaders—taking active initiative to help the organization achieve its goals. Focusing on the good of the whole is an essential survival skill. Such a focus breaks down the *us-versus-them,* management-versus-workers barrier so damaging to trust and morale.

2. Envision Yourself Embodying Learning/Discovery

In Chapters Four through Nine, six components of the Learning/Discovery attitude were described in detail. Now it is time to bring all these ideas together into a coherent picture of the changes you envision for yourself.

Meta-Skill Builder 39: Embracing Learning/Discovery Values

How will you bring Learning/Discovery values into your work? In creating your vision, use the following questions to develop an overall picture of how the six meta-skills can enhance your personal and job effectiveness.

1. How do you see yourself participating with change? What specific things can you do to anticipate change and go out to meet it?

2. How do you see yourself letting go of what you no longer need
—whether it be a belief, a behavior, a project, or a relationship?

3. How do you see yourself expressing your cosmic vocation at
work? And how does this enhance your power and enthusiasm
for what you are doing?

4. With whom do you see yourself communicating with the intent
to know and be known?

5. How do you see yourself using Both/And thinking—and with
what results? Imagine a difficult situation, and see yourself contributing to a solution that all parties can support.

6. How do you see yourself fostering mutual learning in your
groups and teams? What specific contributions would you like
to make?

Once you have articulated your vision, find a trusted friend who
is also familiar with the Learning/Discovery attitude. Invite your
friend to review your vision to see how closely it reflects a value
on learning. Ask this friend to look carefully for subtle indicators of
things like denial, either/or thinking, or the intent to control. When
people have a "foot in both worlds," as we all do in these transi-
tional times, it is impossible to be entirely consistent with one's
stated values. Welcome your friend's feedback as a contribution to
your learning

Ways to Embody the Learning/Discovery Vision

Here are some specific things you can do to embody Learning/
Discovery:

1. You can note how your organization scored in each of the six
meta-skill areas and hold these in mind as you proceed. This helps
you know where the resistances are and where your organization
needs the most help. It can also help you to be realistic about
how your efforts are likely to be received. For example, if your
organization scored low on team learning, do not be disappointed
if you do not get credit for sharing important information with
another project in another department. You might still wish to
share the information, because you have the good of the whole
organization in mind. But do not expect special recognition for
your generosity.

2. In conversations with others, you can ask questions that stim-

ulate Learning/Discovery thinking, such as: "What can we learn from this?" "Who else do we need to include in this decision?" "Is there a way of approaching the problem that is entirely different from the way things have been done before?" "Here is how I see the situation. How do you see it?" "Tell me more about why you see things that way." "How does our work interface with the project that Department T is doing?" "If you could do this job any way you wanted to, how would you approach it?" "Is there anything in this situation that makes it difficult for you to tell me what is really going on with you?" "Do you feel pressure to tell me only the good news?" These questions reveal a wish to understand the situation or the other person more deeply. They build trust because they are motivated by an intent to learn.

3. You can initiate conversations with others about the most satisfying or the most frustrating aspects of their jobs. This helps people get in touch with feelings about the need for change.

4. When someone complains to you about the behavior of another, you can ask if the person in question has been given feedback about this. If the answer is no, you can inquire as to why not. This raises awareness in the informant regarding her resistance. It helps her understand her fears and the possible roots of these fears within the organizational system.

5. You can make a point of noticing peoples' unique talents or essential contributions to a group effort and seek opportunities to mirror this back to them. This can enhance their job satisfaction because they realize that they are expressing a deeper part of themselves in their work.

6. You can identify others in your organization who have a Learning/Discovery orientation. You can informally share knowledge and ideas with these people, thus strengthening the support base in the organization for mutual learning. You can invite some of these people to meet with you on a regular basis for mutual support. (The next section, "Your Support System," explains this in more detail.)

7. You can challenge the unconscious assumptions that often occur in meetings by asking questions such as: "Have we considered and weighed all our options?" "Are we doing it this way because we've always done it this way—or because we think it is the

best plan?" "What leads you to that conclusion?" "Have you checked out that assumption with the appropriate people?"

8. People and groups often resist learning anything really new or transformative due to the belief that "if I admit I don't already know everything, I am somehow inadequate." This belief is behind the "NIH" (Not Invented Here) syndrome—the tendency for systems to reject other people's good ideas because they didn't think of these themselves.

This is the kind of unconscious assumption that needs to be identified and ferreted out of our thinking. It is a belief based on false pride. The NIH mentality is symptomatic of Security/Control thinking.

Look for evidence of this prideful belief in yourself and your organization. If you find it, note its costs. Then engage in informal dialogues with others about your observations. See what you learn about yourself from these conversations. Be careful not to blame your organization. The best way to avoid blaming is to own up to how you personally participate in upholding this norm by conforming to it or by not questioning it.

9. To show others the benefits of learning from experiencing, it helps if you are willing to learn in public. You are not the only one who learns from your mistakes and disappointments. Other people do also. One of your biggest contributions to your organization is your willingness to "live your learning," to try something new, to sometimes fall down, to learn something productive from your fall, and to try again—all in full view of others.

10. If the organization is open to change, you can suggest that an outside organizational consultant (or perhaps an internal consultant from another organization) be called in to assist with the organization's efforts toward self-renewal. A consultant can help you

- define, clarify, and agree upon what changes need to be initiated or how to cope with changes imposed by crisis;
- identify which functional areas need the most work, and which might be good starting points;
- assess the organization's readiness and capability for change;
- create a plan of action that includes long-range goals as well as intermediate and first steps;

- create an in-house team with the skills to carry on the work now begun.

These ten suggestions are things you can begin to do right now to support Learning/Discovery thinking in your workplace. Some of the ideas will feel quite natural to you. Others may not. Just choose the ones that fit your style. Or at least start with those.

3. Your Support System

If you feel deeply connected to Learning/Discovery thinking but are having trouble bringing it into your life as fully as you would like, you probably need a stronger support system to help you.

It is very important to have support when learning a new way of being or thinking. It is almost impossible to sustain significant changes without social support. You need at least one other person who shares your view—preferably more than one. If you work in an organization with fairly low scores in Learning/Discovery, your support system will be all the more important.

Meta-Skill Builder 40: Your Support System

To assess the current and potential support available to you, ask yourself these questions or something similar

1. What does my current support system look like? Who are the significant people in it?
2. Who else among my family, friends, colleagues, or coworkers aspires toward Learning/Discovery thinking?
3. Next to each person's name, note the specific ways these people might be of support or help. Visualize yourself asking for this support. Then visualize yourself receiving it.
4. What groups and organizations could I join or get support from?
5. Are there people or groups at work who might be supportive whom I haven't already named?

How to Develop an Informal Support System Where You Work

It can be very self-empowering to begin meeting informally with others who share your goals or values. This can even be done with coworkers whom you do not know very well.

Don was a high school teacher with a vision for bringing Learning/Discovery values into his school's organizational culture—as a way of helping both the school and himself. He felt a bit like a misfit in the school where he taught. The principal represented Security/Control values like "law and order" and "presenting a united front to the parents." The faculty seemed more interested in controlling students' behavior than in teaching them to think and experiment. Don felt alone and unsupported.

After one particularly disappointing faculty meeting, he and another teacher fell into conversation. They found that they shared certain key values, such as a respect for differences and an interest in promoting teamwork in students. Even though they had no relationship prior to this conversation, they decided to begin meeting together for mutual support. After a few months, two more teachers joined these weekly meetings. The "Gang of Four," as they called themselves, continued to meet after school to share ideas and strategies for creating a more innovative and respectful climate at their school. In their discussions, they created group norms that modeled respectful behavior and contributed to their own self-respect. For example, they took care not to blame or criticize those who did not appear to share their views.

When word got out that the Gang of Four had been having regular meetings for almost a year, some staff members were threatened. This might have created a split in the faculty if the gang had handled it carelessly. As it happened, the gang decided to open one meeting per month to anyone who wanted to attend. This defused the aura of secrecy that others had projected onto them. In time, they dropped the name Gang of Four and began calling themselves the 3 O'clock Bunch. Fortunately, they did such a superb job of making nonmembers feel included that the crisis was averted.

This example highlights a potential danger for your organization. When you create a subgroup to provide mutual support among its members, you need to be mindful of your intent: Is it to unify or to divide, to live Learning/Discovery values or to simply preach them (and perhaps feel a bit superior in the process)? Be careful to envision your purpose as benefiting the group as a whole, and be careful not to inadvertently send the message that everyone should think as you do.

Expect resistance whenever you attempt to introduce any new idea into any system. Try not to resist or resent the resistance you encounter. Rather, see it as a normal part of the change equation, and as information about which parts of the system need extra "hand-holding" or reassurance. And do not see resistance as only belonging to the other. Own up to your own resistance as well. Even when you feel good about making a change or trying something new, there may be some aspects of your personality that move more slowly than other parts. In any system there are fast-changing and slow-changing aspects. Create opportunities for these two sides to stay in respectful dialogue. As we saw in Chapter Eight, this can prevent needless power struggles. Welcome the chance to practice the Both/And attitude with respect to faster and slower-changing parts.

Learning/Discovery Promotes Partnership, Not Paternalism

Throughout this book, we have seen the tremendous cost to organizations arising from the arrogance of power: workers and managers working at cross purposes; management thinking it knows the marketplace without gathering information from those workers who are closest to customers; workers feeling overcontrolled and demoralized. When power and control are the tools for getting the job done, this sets up a mistrustful, adversarial relationship. When mutual learning is the vehicle, relationships become trusting, cooperative, and synergistic.

The paternalism of the past is obsolete. Paternalism arises from the Security/Control attitude, where management thinks it knows best what is good for the rest of the organization.

Partnership is the new organizational form. In partnership, we learn and discover together the best practices and best directions. Everyone feels like an owner of the organization and seeks to serve the common good.

Learning is the great power equalizer. Learning and discovery are available to everyone. With communication technology being what it is today, everyone has access to what is going on, and everyone will have a slightly different perspective on it. This is a great boon to organizational learning. It keeps us humble and open. It keeps us from getting rigid. We know that we will never know all there is to know, that we will always need other peoples' ideas and inputs, and that we never outgrow our need for learning.

As I mentioned in the Introduction, CEOs do not have the complete picture. They need input from stakeholders, just as stakeholders need to feel valued and included. The result of this mutual need is mutual learning, mutual benefit, and mutual empowerment—a sense of partnership.

The ability to facilitate change is an art form. It involves orchestrating divergent impulses or conflicting views into creative solutions. In the Learning/Discovery paradigm, everyone's leadership is needed. Formal leaders need to hold their power in a way that allows room for informal leaders to emerge and be supported. Learning/Discovery fosters shared power and frequent shifts in functional leadership. Nowadays, everyone is part leader and part follower. Regardless of your title, you will find yourself playing different roles, depending on the needs of the situation.

You are well prepared to be this sort of participant-leader if you feel a genuine responsibility for the whole and if you are willing to undergo personal change on a continual basis. In Learning/Discovery, you understand and trust the natural process of change because you are intimately involved in your own personal change. You have the courage and the wisdom to respond to a unique situation in a unique way, rather than according to a predetermined formula or schedule.

In the new workplace, openness and problem-solving skills are more useful than power and control, since one person cannot know the best answer for all. We are learning to be in partnership not only with each other, but also with the constant feedback we get from the situations in which we find ourselves.

Leading is not about getting others to see or do things our way. It is more about facilitating personal and organizational learning—holding up a mirror for ourselves and others so we can see if we are helping or hindering the natural flow of change.

Learning must now become an explicit part of both the individual's and the organization's vision. Even if we aren't sure what a learning organization looks like, even if we fear disappointing ourselves in the quest, we can still set our sights on this vision—the vision of a workplace infused by a passion for learning.

Chapter One

Garvin, David. "Building a Learning Organization." *Harvard Business Review,* Volume 71, Number 4 (1993).

Korn, Lester. *Secrets of a Top Headhunter: How to Get the High-Paying Job You Always Wanted.* New York: Simon & Schuster, 1988.

Naisbitt, John, and Patricia Aburdene. *Megatrends.* New York: William Morrow & Co., 1982.

Toffler, Alvin, and Heidi Toffler. *Futureshock.* New York: Bantam Books, 1971.

————. *Power Shift.* New York: Bantam Books, 1990.

Wriston, Walter. *The Twilight of Sovereignty.* New York: Charles Scribner's Sons, 1992.

Chapter Four

Campbell, Susan. *The Couple's Journey.* San Luis Obispo, Calif.: Impact Publishers, 1980.

Csikszentmihalyi, Mihaly. *Flow.* New York: Harper & Row, 1990.

Chapter Five

Basmajian, John. *Biofeedback: Principles and Practices.* Baltimore: Williams & Wilkins, 1989.

Davis, Martha, Elizabeth Eshelman, and Matthew McKay. *The Relaxation and Stress Reduction Handbook.* Oakland, Calif.: New Harbinger Press, 1988.

Harp, David, with Nina Feldman. *The New Three Minute Meditator.* Oakland, Calif.: New Harbinger Press, 1990.

Juhan, Dean. *Job's Body.* Barrytown, N.Y.: Station Hill Press, 1987.

Klausner, S. Z. *The Quest for Self-Control.* New York: Free Press, 1965.

Marion, Peller. *Crisis-Proof Your Career.* New York: Birch Lane Press, 1993.

Murphy, Michael. *The Future of the Body.* Los Angeles: J. P. Tarcher, 1992.

Needleman, Carla. *The Work of Craft.* New York: Kodansha International, 1993.

Woodman, Marion. *Addiction to Perfection.* Toronto: Inner City Books, 1982.

Chapter Six

Campbell, Joseph. *The Hero with a Thousand Faces.* New York: World Publishing Corp., 1956.

Kouzes, James, and Barry Posner. *The Leadership Challenge.* San Francisco: Jossey-Bass, 1990.

Paul, Margaret. *Inner Bonding: Becoming a Loving Adult to Your Inner Child.* San Francisco: Harper San Francisco, 1990.

Chapter Seven

Anderson, Susan Campbell. "The Effects of Confrontation." *Journal of Counseling Psychology,* Volume 15, Number 5 (1968).

Deming, W. E. *Out of the Crisis.* Cambridge, Mass.: MIT Press, 1986.

Gitlow, Howard, and Shelly Gitlow. *The Deming Guide to Quality Management.* Englewood Cliffs, N.J.: Prentice-Hall, 1987.

Ryan, Kathleen, and Daniel Oestreich. *Driving Fear Out of the Workplace.* San Francisco: Jossey-Bass, 1991.

Chapter Eight

Campbell, Susan. *Beyond the Power Struggle: Dealing with Conflict in Love and Work.* San Luis Obispo, Calif.: Impact Publishers, 1984.

Chapter Nine

Campbell, Susan. *The Couple's Journey.* San Luis Obispo, Calif.: Impact Publishers, 1980.
Senge, Peter. *The Fifth Discipline: The Art and Practice of the Learning Organization.* New York: Doubleday & Co., 1990.

HOW TO RECEIVE SUSAN CAMPBELL'S NEWSLETTER

Susan Campbell and her associates publish a quarterly newsletter, *Uncertain Times,* which offers tools for tapping the creative potential within chaos. To receive a complimentary copy of the newsletter, send your name, address, and phone and fax numbers to:

Susan Campbell, Ph.D.
1740 Brandee Lane
Santa Rosa, CA 95403
(707) 571-7712

Information about speeches, training, and consultation based on the six strategic meta-skills can also be obtained from this address.